ENNISKILLEN:

The Remembrance Sunday Bombing

DENZIL McDANIEL worked for a time in the Civil Service, before leaving to take up a position with *The Impartial Reporter* in Enniskillen. In the 1970s and 1980s he worked on various stories concerning the IRA Border campaign. He has contributed to the English national media and is the Fermanagh correspondent for Downtown Radio.

Enniskillen:

The Remembrance Sunday Bombing

Denzil McDaniel

WOLFHOUND PRESS
& in the US and Canada
The Irish American Book Company

First published in 1997 by
Wolfhound Press Ltd
68 Mountjoy Square
Dublin 1, Ireland
Tel: (353-1) 874 0354
Fax: (353-1) 872 0207

Published in the US and Canada by
The Irish American Book Company
6309 Monarch Park Place
Niwot, Colorado 80503
USA
Tel: (303) 652-2710
Fax: (303) 652-2689

British Library Cataloguing in Publication Data
A catalogue record for this book is available from the British Library.

ISBN 0-86327-611-3

10 9 8 7 6 5 4 3 2 1

Cover Photograph: Gordon Millar, Enniskillen
Cover Design: Slick Fish Design
Typesetting: Wolfhound Press
Printed in the Republic of Ireland by Colour Books, Dublin

Contents

Picture Acknowledgements

Cover photograph, courtesy of Gordon Millar, Enniskillen.

Picture section
Page 1: (top) courtesy of Gordon Millar, Enniskillen; (bottom) courtesy of Raymond Humphreys, Enniskillen.
Pages 2 and 5: courtesy of Raymond Humphreys, Enniskillen.
Page 3: (top) courtesy of the Kennedy family; (middle) courtesy of Stella Robinson; (bottom) courtesy of Margaret Veitch.
Page 4: (top left) portrait of Johnny Megaw, painted by Enniskillen artist Marion Thomson; (top right) courtesy of the Quinton family; (middle left) courtesy of Gladys Gault; (middle right) courtesy of Kathleen Armstrong; (bottom) courtesy of Joan Wilson.
Page 6: (top) courtesy of Austin Stinson; (bottom) courtesy of John McVitty, *Impartial Reporter*, Enniskillen.
Page 7: courtesy of Jim Dixon.
Page 8: (top) photo by Trevor McBride; (bottom) courtesy of Stephen Ross.

Introduction

Like many other things in Northern Ireland, Remembrance Sunday has come to mean different things to different people. For most Protestants, it is exactly what its name implies — a day to remember.

The signing of the Armistice to end the First World War, the 'great war to end all wars', took place at the eleventh hour of the eleventh day of the eleventh month in 1918. In the Allied countries commemorations are held on the nearest Sunday, when successive generations pay homage to those killed in that war, as well as the Second World War and numerous other bloody conflicts.

The First World War was fought before the partition of Ireland, and many thousands of Irishmen from throughout the island lost their lives, suffering heavy losses at the Battle of the Somme in 1916 in particular. The tradition of both Protestants and Catholics joining the British Army to fight a common enemy has continued throughout this century.

However, in Northern Ireland divisions have narrowed perceptions. Now it is mostly Protestants who associate themselves with the British heritage — not exclusively, of course, but enough to instil in many Protestants an increased belief in the importance of symbols such as the red poppy. Although the majority of those who attend the Remembrance Sunday ceremonies are Protestant, many thousands of people from both sides of the divide in Northern Ireland regard the day as a very solemn occasion when people gather in memory of personal friends or family members who paid the supreme sacrifice.

It was this type of ceremony that the IRA attacked in Enniskillen, Co. Fermanagh, in 1987. A bomb killed eleven civilians and injured sixty-three more in what is widely regarded as one of the most appalling of all atrocities. Northern Ireland's 'Troubles' over the past thirty years have produced a macabre list of placenames, which signpost us through the human suffering; the town of Enniskillen's place in history was assured for all the wrong reasons, and the 'Poppy Day bomb' attracted sympathy worldwide.

In writing this book, I was conscious of the need to look at a number of areas, including the significance of the 'Poppy Day bomb' in the context of Northern Ireland's history, and in political terms. I question why it happened and ask whether such a dreadful thing could happen again. But, above all, I examine the real cost of 'Enniskillen' in terms of the human suffering.

1: Day of Carnage

Enniskillen, Co. Fermanagh, is a small market town just inside the Northern part of the Irish Border in south-west Ulster. On 8 November 1987, it was just one venue in one county in Northern Ireland to join communities throughout the United Kingdom in a formal ceremony of laying wreaths of artificial red poppies at the local War Memorial.

Throughout the picturesque island town, people of all ages donned their Sunday best; veterans wore their war medals proudly on the lapel of their 'good suit'; others, including many children, pinned a poppy on their chest. Then they set off, by car or by foot, along the otherwise virtually deserted routes from their homes around the outskirts of the town. Eleven of them never returned.

An Old Sports Bag

The impressive War Memorial, with a distinctive bronze statue of a soldier, was built in 1922, and is a familiar landmark at the east end of the town in the narrow Belmore Street. Unknown to those who gathered, an attack on the ceremony had already been planned. Some time earlier, IRA volunteers had slipped into the area with a bomb, small enough to be carried quite comfortably in an old sports bag.

At the top of Belmore Street, there was a building known locally as the Reading Rooms. The property of St Michael's parish, it used to house the town's Catholic schools, run by the Presentation Brothers. But since new primary, secondary and grammar schools had sprung up in other areas in the 1950s and 1960s, the building had fallen into poor repair. It was still used as a store for camping equipment and canoes for St Michael's Scouts, and in the basement older men would play poker, and youngsters enjoyed snooker and billiards.

The bag, containing forty pounds of explosives, was left on the first floor inside the gable wall which faced onto the War Memorial. It lay unnoticed in a small cupboard on the landing between steps leading to the floor above and another set of steps leading to the basement. An electronic timer on the device was set for just before eleven o'clock.

The Wall of the Reading Rooms

On the Sunday morning, there was a relaxed atmosphere among the people coming to the ceremony. Usually there were about five or six hundred in Enniskillen. Many began arriving up to an hour before the eleven o'clock start, to get a good vantage point.

In 1986 there had been heavy rain — 'coming down like stair rods', as one man recalled in an Enniskillen colloquialism. The wall of the Reading Rooms would provide a little shelter from the west wind and rain, which regularly sweep in from the Atlantic and over the Sligo mountains.

Around the other three sides of the cenotaph, about twenty yards from the wall, others were gathering. By 10.43, almost forty spectators were at the wall, huddled into a stretch of pavement just thirty-five feet long by four feet deep. As they moved in behind a blue steel railing, built to protect pedestrians from passing traffic, greetings were exchanged between friends and neighbours.

Then the bomb timer clicked and the Sunday morning air was filled with the loud explosion. It was a defining moment in the town's history, a split second that would change many lives forever, and a significant event in

Northern Ireland's Troubles, even by their horrible standards.

The wall of the building, well over a hundred years old,
disintegrated and came crashing down on the group of
people standing on the pavement. It came down in large
slabs of masonry, the size of a dinner table. Bricks flew all
around — there were small stone-sized pieces and pounds
and pounds of dust, burying people alive before they
could know what had hit them. The force of the impact
sent people flying against the steel railing, trapping them
tightly, and leaving them with gruesome injuries.

Photographer Gordon Millar was walking up Belmore
Street and watched in horror:

> As you blink, it was just like a big column of smoke going
> straight up and you could actually see the wall. The wall
> just sat for a second and then it started to vibrate. You
> could see it getting a bigger and bigger wobble and then it
> just collapsed. Then it came straight down, just in a heap.

A whoosh of air from the explosion burst out over the east
bridge towards the River Erne, and it seemed as if air
from Belmore Street was sucked into the vacuum in an
instant; panes of glass shattered along the narrow street
as they were pulled out of shop windows onto people
standing around.

In all the eyewitness accounts, there is a remarkable
similarity of description of the next few seconds.

According to Sammy Foster:

> There seemed to be a deathly silence. Then it seemed as if
> all hell broke loose. There was screaming, shrieking, glass
> shattering and breaking, and dust coming all over the
> place.

In the words of Raymond Ferguson:

> There was a period of silence and nobody was quite sure
> what had happened. Suddenly people began to scream
> and panic.

Tommy Halliwell recalls:

There was silence first. Then everybody was shouting at one time. I can remember a cloud of dust and I was crouched down on the ground. I said to Tommy, my lad, 'Are you all right?'

He said, 'I'm okay, Dad.'

I said 'Get the hell out of here, there's a bomb.'

I looked across to the corner, where I'd seen Sammy Gault and others a minute before. Now, I could see nobody at all.

As the reality hit them, Tommy Halliwell and a number of others ran to the collapsed wall and began pulling frantically at the rubble to search for their friends and neighbours. The scenes of pandemonium were captured on video by local businessman Raymond McCartney. At the time, in the shock and confusion, it seemed absurd that someone could continue to record, and Mr McCartney himself is not sure even now why he continued. Later, when Raymond McCartney's vivid pictures were flashed around the world, people were grateful to him for showing the true horror of what had happened.

Rescue Efforts

The true horror was already emerging in the minutes after the bombing as the spontaneous and heroic rescue efforts began. For the next few hours, the only thing on people's minds was the immediate trauma and chaos around the Reading Rooms wall — the eye of the storm where it had become clear that the real damage was.

A couple of dozen soldiers from the Ulster Defence Regiment emerged to delve in the rubble. A prime target for the IRA throughout Northern Ireland's Troubles, they were to have formed a central part of the formal parade to the War Memorial, and 115 men and women from two local companies of 4UDR (Fermanagh) had begun forming up in the car park at the back of the row of shops along Belmore Street.

A Greenfinch (the name given to women soldiers) had been chosen to lay a wreath, and, nervous about it on the drive into town, had turned to her colleague, Private Allen, saying: 'Norman, there's an awful funny feeling in the air today. The shivers are running through me.'

Her feelings were justified. As the column of soldiers in their dress uniform and medals moved off, slightly late because their Commanding Officer had been delayed, the bomb exploded.

Major Kenny Elliott heard the explosion and, knowing that his wife, Heather, had brought their 2-year-old boy to see the parade, instinctively shouted 'Gary'. As he ran up a side street towards the plume of smoke, others were running in the opposite direction, while a few men ran towards the mound of bricks and rubble, and began clawing furiously with their bare hands.

Kenny Elliott remembers:

> What I saw immediately was rough. One poor woman's head was cracked open like a china doll. But there was no great blood and gore, everything was covered in grey dust. This old man looked up at me out of the dust and said 'help me'. A colleague helped me lift a beam off him, but it wasn't an old man, it was Austin Stinson.

Mr Stinson, a local undertaker, aged 24, suddenly found himself buried up to his neck:

> I thought I was dead. I just thought, 'This is it, I am dead and they are taking me away.' It was really crazy. I was trapped — there was a big boulder on my legs, my hair was all dust. I was trapped up to my neck. My head wasn't buried, that was one thing. But I definitely thought I had died, that's the truth. There was somebody down underneath the rubble in front of me in a black coat and I was pulled out over the top of somebody else.

Austin Stinson quickly realised that he was not dead:

> I was one of the first taken out. The UDR boys pulled me over to the bridge and I said, 'I'm all right; leave me alone and go and see somebody else.'

He tried to get up but could not — his pelvis was broken.

Kenny Elliott shouted out, to no one in particular, 'We

need help!' and turned to see what he describes as 'a sea of khaki' of UDR men running towards the rubble. One of them stood back and shouted, 'Watch for the double tap.'

British troops training for service in Northern Ireland are warned to guard against a 'secondary device' in terrorist attacks. In 1979, at Warrenpoint in Co. Down, troops rushed in too quickly to the scene of a bombing, lured into the trap of a second bomb. A total of eighteen soldiers were killed.

However, while one man at Enniskillen remembered his military training, his call was given short shrift by his colleagues — the UDR is a regiment made up almost entirely of local men and women. Like Kenny Elliott, many of them knew the people they were digging out, and dreaded that their loved ones would be among them.

Civilians were helping, too. Tommy Halliwell was pulling with his bare hands:

> Everybody was the same You just get stuck in and do what you have to do. It could be a mother, brother, sister, anybody lying in there. They need help but you don't think, you just do it. We were just throwing the rubble back and it was the wrong thing to do because we were just hitting the people behind with it. Then somebody shouted to throw the rubble the other way, out over the wall towards the river.
>
> The first body I saw was Johnny Megaw. We lifted Johnny and Ted Armstrong — at the time we didn't know who at first, your mind was playing tricks. We lifted Johnny Megaw and put him on the pavement. The next one was Ted Armstrong. His coat was blew inside out ... his overcoat ... unbelievable ... he had a big heavy black coat and it was blown inside out. Then we got Sammy Gault. Sammy was in tight to the fence, but we got him out. His watch was still going.

These three men were clearly dead, and as more bodies were pulled out, rescuers laid them down on the street a few yards away and returned to the scene of carnage. RUC men whipped off their overcoats and hurriedly covered the faces of the dead. But they were still easily identifiable as bodies: limbs protruded from under the makeshift covers, and people searching for missing relatives would briefly lift the covers. One woman was heard to cry 'It's him, it's him', but on discovering that it was not her relative, she screamed even louder.

Tommy Halliwell continued working:

> I was standing on a big slab of masonry or something. Somebody said, 'We'll have to get that out of the road.' It was so big that we had to get help to lift it. Underneath is where young Ross was lying. He was actually under it; how that cub survived I do not know.

In Fermanagh slang, boys are fondly called 'cubs' and girls are 'cutties'. The 'cub' Ross was 15-year-old Stephen Ross. Now working near Basingstoke in the south of England, Stephen Ross remembers with remarkable clarity the moments after the bomb:

> I had a pair of navy trousers on and a navy and green jumper. I was wearing a pair of shoes I'd bought recently which I was quite proud of. I was standing holding my 12-year-old sister Catherine's hand. All of a sudden an explosion went off. It was a horrendous noise; the second it happened, I knew straight away what it was.
>
> The next thing I remember is being pulled out of the rubble. I couldn't see a thing. I couldn't feel my left leg at all below my knee and I just remember tasting dust and blood in my mouth and putting my hand in my mouth and finding that most of my front teeth had gone. I tried to open my eyes but I just couldn't see anything: all I could do was hear the noise, taste the dust — that gritty cement dust — taste blood in my mouth. All I could hear was people screaming and shouting.

Stephen's sister received head injuries as well. Their father, Graham Ross, found her quite quickly but faced a frantic few hours searching for Stephen, who he finally found later that day at the Erne Hospital. Stephen's face was a mess and he still had months of treatment to endure. But he was one of the lucky ones.

Bodies Unrecognisable

Ten people were already dead, one more would die later. A total of sixty-three were injured, the most serious injuries being suffered by those buried in the rubble. Many of the dead were unrecognisable even to close friends.

Ulster Unionist member of Fermanagh District Council, Sammy Foster, has attended Enniskillen's Remembrance Sunday almost every year since 1953 to honour family members killed in war. In 1987, he was there in an official capacity, standing with other members of the local council on the other side of the Memorial, outside O'Doherty's butcher's shop. He remembers the bomb going off:

> I hit the ground and curled up like a snail covering my head. When things quelled I didn't know where the bomb was. I turned round, looking through my fingers — it was like looking through a smoke-filled room. The first man I saw was Henry Keys, the Model School principal, with a child under each arm, coming out of it. I said, 'Are they okay, Henry?'
>
> He said, 'They're okay physically, but they're badly shaken up.'

Mr Foster joined the rescue efforts at the wall.

> We tried to lift the gable wall. It was too heavy for us. This bloke to my right was bleeding profusely from the mouth, I put my hand under his chin, my hand was red with blood. I didn't know who he was at the time: everybody was pallor-like with the dust and fright. There was a lady to my left. I thought at first it was Mrs John Irvine. It wasn't. Then I thought it was Mrs Alfie Scollan. Turned out it was Sister Quinton.
>
> I put my hand under this other bloke who turned out to be Wesley Armstrong. I put my hand under his chin and my other hand just as consolation under the lady's head. I'm sure I could see the body colour changing as if death was coming through her body. I reckon the woman was dead even when I had my hand on her head.

This was Alberta Quinton, a much-loved retired nurse,

known to friends as Alberta or 'Bertha', and to others simply as 'Sister'.

Paramedics came with breathing apparatus and put it on Wesley Armstrong's mouth. Sammy Foster continued to support Wesley, with his hand under his chin, until Dr McVeigh arrived from the hospital and said: 'Sammy, let him go, he's gone.' Mr Foster can still feel 'his dying shudder'. Beside Wesley, his wife Bertha also lay dead.

Orphaned

Remarkably, Wesley and Bertha Armstrong's 16-year-old son, Julian, who was standing between them, survived. For some time afterwards, his older sisters were concerned that he would not talk about his experience. But he did so in his own time and now, ten years on, it is impossible not to be impressed by his strength and calm.

I remember when we got there behind the blue railing. I remember walking up to it. My dad was holding an umbrella and my mother had a blue coat on. She was wearing her glasses. I remember Mum waving to someone, I think it was Angel Robinson. And that split second the wall came down. I was holding on to the railing and just felt all this rubble coming on my back.

I just pulled myself up with all my strength; I was determined to get up from that rubble. I thought, 'I must look for my parents.' I went straight to my mum first, looked at my dad and he was under a big slab of concrete. I then looked at my mum, then pulled all these bricks off my mum and threw them out as quick as possible. I just looked at my mum and knew she was dead. Her face was totally squashed. I don't think anyone should have seen that in their life because she was in a pretty bad state. It was like a big horror movie nightmare to see my mother like that.

Then I looked at my dad and he had a big slab of concrete. He was looking to me at the side, and the concrete was so heavy I just couldn't lift it. I tried to lift it and then he just shook out in front of me. I think when people die they just shake like that when the life is going out of them.

I had a cut on my ear and later I had a neck brace on. I had a few cuts and bruises on my legs, that's all.

Julian was conscious throughout.

Organised Chaos

Rescue efforts continued for over an hour. In what one man described as 'organised chaos', there was an invisible curtain dividing two worlds. On one side, under the rubble, were the dead and injured; just a few feet away were soldiers, policemen, local people and members of bands in the uniform they were supposed to parade in.

Ballyreagh Silver Band had led the Enniskillen parade every year for almost four decades. Renowned in the area, the youths and young women, as well as the older men, took pride in their music and in their green and red uniforms. They were slightly late in 1987. Bandmaster Robin Emerson had forgotten his music and had to go back. Drummer Freddie Millar, then aged 63, remembers waiting in the car park with other band members when, 'Up she went. All I could see was dust.' He dropped his drum and ran, still in his hand the drumsticks kept as a memento of his time playing in the Army band in 1953. He still has the drumsticks, having subconsciously handed them to Mervyn Farrell to mind, while he helped Tommy Halliwell to lift out Sergeant Gault.

Sammy Gault was covered with a blanket. Meanwhile, his son Keith was on his way over the bridge thirty yards away with his new baby.

Freddie Millar continued to pull at the rubble:

Then we found Kenneth McBrien, who I was at school with. But I couldn't recognise him; he was shouting, 'My leg's off.' We pulled his son, Peter, out too.

In fact, despite the pain and some terrible injuries, Mr McBrien had not lost his leg.

Freddie Millar, Sammy Foster and others then helped to pull out Jim Dixon. Sammy recalls:

Me and Albert Devers, four of us pulled rubble from around this individual and got him out. I didn't even know the man. But, as we say in Fermanagh, he was a rickle of bones, this poor creature being pulled out. Turned out it was Jim Dixon. I did know Jim from before but I didn't know him then. Jim's still suffering; he has great drive and motivation. If he was a lesser individual, he would be gone by now.

Jim Dixon, then aged 50, recalls the day that he aged years:

It was a cold day and I didn't have a coat. I walked past Johnny Megaw and Mr Mullan (both later killed) and had just went to the end of the railings at the telephone box, past where they were all killed. I looked over and saw Mr Hill standing in his black coat and black gloves. I said to my wife, 'He's lonely looking. We'll go over and chat him.'

I had my camera with me — I was going to take a photograph of my daughter laying the wreath — and we had taken about two steps from the railing, which may have saved our lives.

I heard something [at this point, Mr Dixon made a clicking noise with his tongue]. It was probably the detonator going off. The bomb would have done an awful lot more harm if they hadn't set it on a wooden floor. The building fell, collapsed rather than blown out. If it had been blown out it could have killed hundreds of people, especially if the full crowd had've been gathered. But the parade was late that day.

The bomb blew my wife a number of feet away but I was struck on the head, on the side of the face, which did a lot of damage, and part of the building fell on my body and smashed my pelvis and hips and leg.

He remembers drifting in and out of consciousness and thinking, 'I am not too good.'

I remember putting my hand up to my face and the blood was flying out of my jaw. My jaw on this side was missing — that is the side that got the blast. I thought I must be badly hurt and I had no pain at that stage. It was just like hell.

His wife, Anna, had escaped serious injury. The buttons were blown off her coat and the shoes off her feet. But apart from a few bumps, she was all right. She pulled herself out of the rubble and immediately began to look for her husband.

Calling on God

Mrs Dixon recalls:

> I recognised his suit. I remember seeing his face and saying, 'We are going to be all right.' But then I was screaming and screaming, I couldn't stop screaming. There was a deathly silence, I almost felt that there was just Jim and me there. It was terrifying. I remember trying to pray, looking up into the heavens, the sky and trying to call on God and being very aware that I couldn't find God. I felt evil, a sense of evil around me. That was a terrifying experience and I often think about it, to think I was standing there and not being able to find God. I am not comparing myself to Jesus, but I can almost relate to what He said on the Cross, 'My God, My God, why hast Thou forsaken me?'
>
> Then a girl ran across the road, she didn't know she was coming particularly to me. She put her arms around me and prayed and when she prayed I felt that evil lifting.

She was with her husband as the men pulled him out. Nuns began arriving to help. Anna Dixon told a nun to go away. Mr Dixon says:

> We know the history of the Catholic Church, what the aims and objectives are and have been for 600 years. We are not talking personal figures in this, but to be assisted by someone who is party to what has gone on we would find very obnoxious. When they came to help my wife she was very antagonistic.

Uncomfortable as it may make us feel, in the divided society of Northern Ireland, a certain strand of fundamentalist Christians view the Catholic Church as the personification of evil. It might be very much a minority view, but it is there, and in this incidence, in the middle of the chaos of a bomb, it came out. The nun, Sister Ann Marie, quickly moved on. She remembers the shock she felt as she realised that someone associated her with the bomb:

> I saw the whole struggle in her face and I suddenly real-ised I was dressed in my religious habit, my sisters' habit. I could see what was happening: she couldn't make any sense of why I was there. I think in her mind she was linking me with the bombing and I got an awful shock be-cause I thought, 'Oh God, she is linking me with what happened.' Just the thought that I could be linked in any-body's mind with murder and violence gave me a shock.

About twenty yards past the bombed building is the local convent, home to almost twenty nuns, mostly teachers or retired teachers. They joined the rescue effort, bringing blankets down from the convent and helping people into nearby homes. Sister Ann Marie lived in the convent. Principal of St Fanchea's girls' school in Enniskillen, she had dressed in her religious habit that morning, to leave for the funeral of a close family friend in Glasgow. She was with Sister Mary when the bomb went off, and they dashed down the avenue. She found it difficult to make sense of the scene they encountered:

> This is as clear to me as if it was yesterday. I remember it was so dark — there was black, black smoke. I wondered where all the people were because I had seen a lot of people gathering earlier on.

She remembers that ambulances began arriving as she went over to a woman to help her. Television viewers watching the footage of the scenes — those who knew the nuances of the occasion — found it strange to see a glimpse of a nun in her habit in the middle of an event that had, over the years, become a predominantly Protes-tant occasion.

The Cavanaghs, the Armstrongs and Pat O'Doherty, who lived above his butcher's shop, were also helping out, although distressed themselves.

In time, it became clear that the vast majority of Protestants held no ill will towards their Catholic neighbours.
They were able to differentiate quite clearly between the
Catholic community and those who had carried out the
attack.

A Bond in Adversity

A young policewoman was taking real physical risks to
clamber in under the rubble to comfort an elderly woman.
The policewoman, Ann McElwaine, and the woman, Lily
Irvine, now aged 77, forged a bond in adversity and are
still firm friends.

Ann remembers people crying and moaning:

> I just went where I could see people who were in need of
> help and helped this woman in particular whose hands
> were coming out through the railing. It was Lily Irvine. I
> more or less did first aid and kept her talking to keep her
> conscious. She was actually lying flat on the ground, the
> rubble was piled up among other people who were injured
> and dead above her.

Mrs Irvine still suffers from pain in her leg. She had been
standing beside her husband, John, who is now 90 years
old and suffers from Parkinson's Disease. 'The doctors
say the bomb didn't help him,' according to Lily who
recalls the day:

> My head was pushed up against the railing, my face went
> kind of crooked. The hairdresser said to me the other day,
> 'I see you still have your wee mark on your head.' A big
> plank fell on my legs, I've arthritis in my two knees. I have
> to take six tablets in the morning and five at night. John
> just got a scratch on his hand. Bertha [Sister Quinton] was
> beside me and Kit came down over the top of me.

Kit Johnston was dead, as was his wife, Jessie. Their
bodies were removed by rescuers and laid out gently.
Similarly the bodies of William and Nessie Mullan, who
had been standing at the end of the footpath which leads
down to the Queen Elizabeth Road, away from Belmore

Street. The Mullans were standing with their backs against the wall, where they could see the young people ready to lay wreaths, among them their 10-year-old grandson, Adam, standing across from them with his school principal, Henry Keys.

Policemen such as Glen Parkes and Sean Harland were doing what they could. There were now ten bodies. The smoke and dust had settled a bit, but the cries continued. It was expected that there would be more bodies, and people were feverishly searching for relatives. UDR soldier Roy Scollan saw a hand sticking out. He thought he recognised a ring that he'd bought his mother, and the colour of the coat was the same as hers too. He pulled off the bricks and stones but it was not her. Somebody else had lost their mother.

Another UDR man noticed a gloved hand and began digging to bring out Ronnie Hill, the headmaster of Enniskillen High School, who had been standing close to young people from his Bible class at the Presbyterian Sunday School.

Some of the UDR people were trained in first aid — in fact, a few months before, they had won a Northern Ireland competition. Ambulance man Albert Devers, who had been down to watch the parade, was using his training too. But probably the most valuable medical work in the immediate minutes after the explosion was done by an off-duty British soldier, Captain Iain McDonald. A qualified nurse from the Royal Army Medical Corps, he was attached to the Fermanagh UDR as their medical officer. In the war along the Border he had gained a lot of experience in dealing with the effects of the bomb and the bullet. He was at the parade in civilian clothes, but the rattle of plastic in his coat pockets as he walked was a supply of airways — little tubes that were to prove invaluable. The condition of many victims was complicated by the effects of dust and smoke, so he worked on a number to insert an airway to keep them breathing.

The digging continued amid a range of emotions, ranging from shock to determination. The soundtrack of the videotape is punctuated with one man's cry of 'The bastards', while an army officer barks out instructions. The footage shows members of the UDR band in their brown kilts, and a number of RUC men and women. One of their colleagues — 29-year-old George Evans — looks in great distress as he is gingerly lifted out. He turned out to be one of the worst affected, but remembers nothing of the incident.

The Walking Wounded

As people were rescued, they were taken the short distance — less than a mile — to the town's Erne hospital. Ambulances had arrived, people were being ferried in police cars and private vehicles. Some even walked.

All age groups had been injured. Seventy-four-year-old Dick Thompson and his 68-year-old wife Dora were badly injured; another married couple brought to hospital were Alan and Daphne Stephenson, in their thirties. Gordon Wilson had received injuries to his left shoulder. A local draper, he had been standing waiting for the ceremony beside his 20-year-old daughter, Marie. Within a day, his famous interview would thrust him before the world media.

Rescuers pulled the bricks and masonry away from the lower half of his body, and retired policeman Sam Murray brought him over to sit down on the kerb at the cenotaph.

Sam had been with his wife, Phyllis, at the other side of the Memorial when the bomb went off. Having attended to a little girl cut by glass beside him, he hurried over to where he had seen his friends, Sammy Gault, Kit and Jessie Johnston and Ted Armstrong, a few minutes before:

> I saw the whole thing happening; I actually saw the wall falling out, it dropped down on top of them. I went over to the corner, but I don't think I should be mentioning who I saw or what I saw because it was fairly gruesome.

By the time he got to Gordon Wilson, he was sitting on top of the rubble:

> When I got to him there were a couple of boys working at him, but he wasn't even up to his waist at that stage. He was just trapped by the legs. I was taking him down to set him down at the cenotaph and he said 'You're hurting my arm.' He walked over with me and I got a police car to bring him to the hospital.

Raymond Ferguson also remembers seeing Gordon Wilson. An Ulster Unionist councillor, Raymond was due to lay the wreath on behalf of Fermanagh District Council. He recalls the mêlée as he joined people trying to help:

> I can remember Gordon Wilson when he came out, sitting on the cenotaph steps. He clearly was in some distress.

While Gordon Wilson's injuries were relatively minor, his daughter Marie was in a bad way. She was alive when rescuers got to her, but UDR soldiers remember her saying, 'There's a wee boy under there; leave me alone and get him.' This concern for others was a common reaction among many of the victims at the scene and at the hospital.

The digging continued for nearly two hours. One man had the presence of mind to remember that he had seen a mechanical digger in another part of town, where a local engineering firm had been carrying out work. The digger was brought up to the site, although in the early stages it was of limited use because too many people were still underneath. But it did help to lift some of the very heavy slabs.

Children in Terror

There has always been a high proportion of children at Enniskillen's ceremony, many in the uniform of church youth organisations such as the Scouts and Guides, Boys Brigade and Girls Brigade. Others represent their schools, and many stand in groups, separated from their parents.

What I remember most of all about the scene was the sheer terror of children searching for their parents and parents in an awful state looking for their children. I lived less than half a mile from the cenotaph on a hill overlooking the town. I didn't hear the bomb go off, just the back door rattling. Within seconds, my sister-in-law rang to say that smoke was coming from the cenotaph. I dashed down.

My colleague, Raymond Humphreys, was already there. The photographer on *The Impartial Reporter*, he covered the event every year. When he had found his children, Carol-Ann and Jonathan, his journalistic instincts took over and he began to take photographs. His pictures, along with those of UDR photographer Gordon Millar and Raymond McCartney's video, vividly show the immediate effects of terrorism.

Bandsman Freddie Millar's wife recalls seeing:

> the wee girl [Julie] Bracken, her shoes blown off and her feet streaming with blood. She was hysterical looking for her brother, he was up in the hospital.

Local businessman David Stuart was seen 'running up the street with one of the kids under his arm like a bag of potatoes and another one over his shoulder.'

Children were witnessing horrific scenes that will stay with them for ever. One Boys Brigade member later said:

> At the time we went to remember our dead, we didn't expect to be digging them out.

The Final Death Toll

As troops and policemen on duty continued to move people back, the digging continued at the rubble for over an hour. It was feared that there could be more dead.

Joan Trimble lives overlooking the scene. She remembers hearing the bomb and going to the bedroom window, from where she saw smoke rising and swirling and filling the whole area. A neighbour, Conor Magee, went past and she shouted, 'What's happened?'

'It's bad; they must all be killed,' he replied.

As the military took over, Raymond Ferguson went to a telephone to contact home, as many others were doing too:

> I knew they would be hearing it on the news. As the day went on, people were asking who had been killed. There was talk about 25, 30 and then it came down to 17 or 18. Then it came down to late that night it was clarified at around 11.

Indeed, it is remarkable that the death toll was not higher. Looking at the area of footpath where the group of people stood, what is particularly striking is that certain individuals escaped with little more than a scratch, while standing beside someone who was killed. It was also providential that most of those who died were in middle or older age, although mingled throughout the group were a number of teenagers who all survived. Stephen Gault, just 18, was standing beside his father Sammy Gault who died. Stephen was thrown out over the railing. Julian Armstrong, aged 16, was between his parents who were both killed. Another 16-year-old, Clive Armstrong, had been standing beside his father, Ted Armstrong, but moved over a little to talk with a group of teenagers, Stephen and Catherine Ross, Nathan Chambers and Ian Carson. According to his mother, Clive was 'found down at the water's edge with the suit just tore off his back.'

Nathan Chambers celebrated his fifteenth birthday two days before the bomb. He remembers leaving Mr Hill's Bible class with the others and standing with his friends at the Memorial:

> There was a loud thud, and then complete blackness. I didn't know what had happened. I had been blown to the ground and curled up in a ball. I realised I was sort of semi-covered in rubble. I lifted myself and pushed the rubble off. I tried to walk, but couldn't. Then I looked down and my left leg was broken and badly twisted.

Nathan's brother, Stephen, was in another area and saw what happened. He dashed to the Presbyterian church where his father and mother, Ronnie and Irene Chambers, were finishing their Sunday School classes. Ronnie ran to the rubble and began digging along with other rescuers. But by then Nathan had already been put in the back of somebody's car and been brought to hospital, where he was soon to be reunited with his relieved parents.

In the words of Gladys Gault, 'Fathers were taken, but the children were spared.'

A number of adults, such as Harry Donaldson and Vernon Huey, received pelvic injuries, and June McIlfatrick was hit on the head. While the most serious casualties were at the wall, there were many injured within a radius of fifty yards of the seat of the explosion. May Stinson, Pearl Cathcart and Margaret Elliott were members of the Women's Section of the Royal British Legion, and had been standing together. When the bomb went off, Margaret was left holding a pane of glass which fell out of a shop window. Sitting on top of it was May's handbag.

Paying Homage

The search continued against the backdrop of the wooden skeleton of the Reading Rooms roof, and the security operation was already under way to seal off the area. By lunchtime the world knew and was horrified by what had happened at Enniskillen. The focus of attention moved elsewhere: to the hospital and the homes around the town where relatives were coming to terms with the bombing of people who had gathered to pay homage on Remembrance Sunday.

That homage was paid. A small group of survivors had moved along the several hundred yards to the other end of Belmore Street where there was another, lesser-known, stone memorial. In the group were several schoolchildren and Royal British Legion president Ronnie Towers, still wearing his black bowler hat, which was now, like his suit, covered in white dust. Somehow, they gathered their thoughts and silently laid their poppy wreaths there, while Ballyreagh Silver Bandsman David Fyffe played the last post — the noise of the bugle mingling with the noise of the digging at the other end of the street.

2: Dead or Alive?

While the bomb took a split second to detonate, and the most intense rescue efforts lasted just over an hour, the repercussions spread worldwide and are still being felt. By Sunday lunchtime, the circle of impact had already widened to take in the whole town. Most immediately, attention shifted to the small Erne hospital, where staff were suddenly coping with a disaster of major proportions. The effects were also being felt in the various churches where services were due to start.

The nearest church, the Presbyterian, was barely a hundred yards away, and already the young minister, the Rev. David Cupples, was arriving to find his people in a state of shock. They were soon to find out that they had been hit the hardest, with six of the eleven dead coming from their congregation.

After the ceremony in Belmore Street, the parade should have made its way up through the town centre's series of winding and hilly main streets, each one following the other seamlessly to form one long main thoroughfare. The parade of bands, war veterans, UDR soldiers and standard-bearers usually makes its way to St Macartin's Church of Ireland cathedral where the main service of remembrance is held, with members of the Royal British Legion taking part.

The Rector, Canon John McCarthy, heard the bomb as he was chatting to the Primate of the Church of Ireland, Archbishop Robin Eames, who was to be the guest preacher that day. The two men rushed to the hospital to comfort the injured and bereaved, while the Bishop of Clogher, the Right Rev. Brian Hannon, went into the cathedral to pray briefly with a stunned congregation. One of the women acting as usher that morning was Gladys Gault. She too had heard the bomb but had no way of knowing that her husband was dead.

Across the way at the Methodist church, Gordon Wilson's wife, Joan, had come down from her home to play the organ at the service.

In between the Methodist building and the Church of Ireland cathedral is sandwiched St Michael's Roman Catholic church where several hundred people were attending eleven o'clock Mass. The parish priest, Monsignor Seán Cahill, hurriedly prepared a brief statement informing them of what he called the 'massacre of the innocents'. Many of his parishioners filed out in silent disbelief and made their way down the hill, some heading towards the Cornagrade, Hillview and Kilmacormick housing estates. On their way, they passed the Erne hospital, where the battle to save lives was being fought.

Hospital Alert

It had been a typical, quiet Sunday morning at the 113-bed district hospital, where staff cover was minimal, especially in the deserted casualty area. In the whole hospital there were three surgical doctors along with one staff nurse and a plaster orderly in casualty, while also on site looking after all the patients were one medical registrar, two medical house officers and an anaesthetist, together with twenty nursing staff, one of whom was a nursing auxiliary.

Malcolm Brown, research registrar at Queen's Department of Surgery in Belfast, was down in Enniskillen on his second weekend covering for senior surgeon Andrew McKibben who was taking some time off. Mr Brown had just checked on a patient in surgical with a problem in her toe, when he heard what he describes as a 'muffled crump'.

A patient looked out the window and saw smoke coming from the War Memorial. The staff quickly went on full-scale alert. An emergency call came in within minutes; one ambulance driver was on site and he was quickly dispatched. A second crew reported in quickly, and two mini-buses were sent as it became apparent that there was a major incident. Mr Brown swiftly moved down the corridors to casualty. It was now empty but would soon be overflowing, with patients even being treated on the floor.

A 'disaster plan' had been drawn up by the hospital administrators with the help of social services, the army and police officers who had visited the local Territorial Army base on the west side of town. It had been updated just three weeks before the day of the bomb. Now it was brought into action as those 'dead on arrival' at the hospital were immediately sent on to a large empty garage at the TA base, chosen to be used as a makeshift mortuary.

At 11.03 a.m., twenty minutes after the explosion, the first casualties arrived at the Erne. Malcolm Brown's job was to implement a 'triage' — making quick assessments of the dozens of injured, and dividing them into three categories. Those whose condition did not appear serious or life-threatening could wait; those already dead were sent on to the mortuary; while those struggling for their lives were worked on urgently.

Mr Brown says that the nature of the bomb and the bomb site almost assisted him in the triage:

> The most seriously injured were the last to come in because they were the ones who were trapped under the rubble. First to arrive were people who were more or less walking wounded, so we were able to put them into the physiotherapy and outpatients departments. There were a few nurses around who comforted and gave them painkillers, explaining they would have to wait because at that stage we really didn't know how many people we were going to get.

Then came the people with more serious injuries:

> It was like a battlefield, there was no doubt about it. The
> little resuscitation area was only geared for four patients;
> we threw the trolleys out because they were cluttering the
> area. We put patients on the floor, so in the area where
> there were normally four, we had eight or nine major
> casualties.

Hospital staff who had been off-duty were pouring in.
They had either heard the bomb or seen it on the television news. Thirteen more surgeons appeared, as did
thirty-seven additional nursing staff, including a local
health visitor and a school nurse. Four local GPs came
along and opened the next-door health centre to treat
those with cuts and bruises.

Just as rescuers at the site were digging for friends
and neighbours, hospital staff were almost all local too.
Many staff, already struggling to cope with the practical
and logistical difficulties, gasped as they recognised
neighbours coming in. In this respect, Malcolm Brown's
job was less traumatic:

> It was a bit easier for me because I was an outsider as it
> were. I remember the comments from the nursing staff:
> 'Oh, I know who that is.' They had the problem, too, when
> the relatives of seriously injured people were coming in.
> They had to keep the relatives calm, knowing what was
> going on to their nearest and dearest. I think they did a
> marvellous job because it was very difficult for them.

Within a few hours, there were over a hundred patients
and relatives in the hospital. Mr Brown continues:

> We had a lot of very brave people. I remember patients
> who were extremely badly injured who were extremely good
> and calm. There was no hysterics from the patients and
> they were very tolerant. The children were remarkable. A
> lot of them had major cuts, bruises and broken bones, all
> extremely happy just to think they were out of it.

The hospital's consultant surgeon, Andrew McKibben,
was alerted. He came in and remained in theatre from

lunchtime until nine o'clock that evening. He recalls:

> There were some harrowing scenes. What was particularly difficult was that I knew many of the people, and word kept coming in of those who died and I knew them too. But your professional training takes over, and it's only afterwards you feel the emotion.

Two theatres remained in action all day.

Airlifted to Derry and Belfast

Despite the troubled history of Northern Ireland, it was unusual for a small-town hospital to have to deal with such a situation. Where the bombing campaign in the 1970s had caused multiple casualties, the bombs tended to be in places such as Belfast where major hospitals were reasonably close. As the more serious injuries came into the Erne, those with severe facial and chest injuries were transferred quickly to bigger hospitals in Belfast and Derry. Army helicopters were used, some of them too big to land on the hospital's small helipad, so the nearby Gaelic football field was used as a landing area.

In casualty, the extent of Jim Dixon's injuries was becoming clear. He was drifting in and out of consciousness, and had to be taken by helicopter to the Altnagelvin hospital in Derry, where he needed nine hours of surgery. As he was leaving the helicopter, Mr Dixon regained consciousness and told paramedics, 'If you can't stop me shaking, I am going to die.' He recalls:

> They cut whatever was covering me and rolled me in aluminium foil. Within two minutes my temperature went from zero; it was like going into an oven at about 90 degrees. It was marvellous, it was a life saver.

Ronnie Hill, the man Jim Dixon had been intending to go over and chat to just before the bomb went off, also had to be transferred. The headmaster of Enniskillen High School, Mr Hill was still conscious in the hours immediately after the bomb. His wife, Noreen, had not been with him that day — she was recovering from cancer and had finished a course of chemotherapy in September. She remembers hearing the explosion:

> I was at home when it went off. I knew it was a bomb and I knew Ronnie was injured. I started to cry and Siobhan [her 17-year-old daughter] came downstairs. I said there was a bomb at the cenotaph and she said, 'No Mum, it's a gun salute.' She was trying to protect me because I was in such a state.

Telephone lines were down, making it difficult for people to get information, so many of them simply headed for the Erne. At the hospital, Mrs Hill learnt that her sixth sense had been correct. She recalls her initial feelings on seeing her badly injured husband for the first time:

> I think you are so relieved to see him that you don't take it in. He looked like an old man, he was grey from top to toes and he had two great plums where his eyes should have been. He was able to speak a little but not very much because he had a fractured jaw. He went in and had his X-rays and after a short time in the ward was airlifted to Altnagelvin.

In the hospital in Derry, Mrs Hill was told that her husband had a fractured skull, fractured jaw, fractured shoulder and fractured pelvis. He had thirty-seven stitches to the face, but the most serious damage was caused by bomb-blast lung — two days later, on the Tuesday, he slipped into a coma. He has not regained consciousness in the ten years since the bomb.

The third patient to be airlifted from Enniskillen to Derry on Sunday afternoon was teenager Stephen Ross. His mother rushed out of the house 'in total panic' to search for her three children, 15-year-old Stephen, 12-year-old Catherine and Rosemary who was 10. Mrs Ross and her husband, Graham, could not find Stephen who says:

> They nearly had to resort to going through those that were killed in the explosion to try and find me. It was at

least an hour and a half, it was quite a shock to them. The only thing I remember seeing was my father's face. I just remember opening my eyes and I said 'Hello' and he said, 'You don't know how glad I am to see you.' I have a good pair of lungs and my father said he has never heard anybody scream as loud as I did.

Virtually all the bones in Stephen's face were broken and the roof of his mouth was split from front to back. He had to have five and a half hours of specialist surgery later that night to rebuild his face.

Some of the injured were being transferred to hospitals in Belfast. Sixty-eight-year-old Dora Thompson had seventeen fractures to her ribs, a broken collar bone, and fractures to her arms, legs and kneecap. Her lung had also collapsed. She spent five weeks in intensive care in Belfast.

Young policeman George Evans appeared more concerned with the condition of others when he arrived at hospital. His wife, Veronica, was sitting by his bedside when she noticed his pupils dilating, and called a nurse. It was quickly realised that his head injury was serious, and he was rushed to Belfast.

There was no time to transfer Marie Wilson — by the time the young nurse arrived at the Erne, her heart had already stopped. She was resuscitated before surgeons brought her straight to theatre, struggling for four hours to keep her alive.

Searching for Marie

In common with many other relatives, at this stage, Marie's family did not know where she was. Even her father, Gordon, who was being treated in another part of the hospital, had no idea that his daughter was in theatre, fighting for her life. Her mother, Joan, was in town at the Methodist church, where she was due to play the organ.

Also due to attend the service was David Bolton, a social worker, who decided to drive over to the hospital to lend assistance and to find information to relay to anxious relatives such as Mrs Wilson. He remembers:

> It was like walking into another world. I felt I was walking
> into something that was just going to be awful and I took
> this desire to run away; but I knew I wouldn't. It was like
> a field hospital. I was amazed at the commitment and se-
> riousness on the faces of the nurses and doctors. There
> was a tremendous sense of people weeping and moaning,
> and in the midst of all that, people scurrying about and
> people coming with drips and blood, running to labs, and
> people being dashed to X-ray. It was utterly chaotic, but
> there was a tremendous sense of purpose about it.

The senior nurse on duty, Ethel Dundas, was remaining
calm, adopting the attitude that the situation was one
that staff could not control, so all they could do was
accept things, and support people where possible. She
recalls that by far the hardest thing to cope with was
telling relatives that a loved one had been killed or very
seriously injured. Relatives were clamouring for information, which sometimes simply was not available. The area
was covered in dust and dirt, as were the patients, and
many were almost unrecognisable. Policeman Clive
Johnston helped to restore some order by providing vital
information from a list of names on his clipboard.

David Bolton phoned back to church to say that he
had found Gordon Wilson. Joan Wilson had begun to play
the organ at the church, but fifteen minutes into the
service she was thinking, 'I just can't do it any more.'
Just then, a UDR man came over and whispered, 'Mrs
Wilson, come with me. Gordon is in the hospital and he
has a broken arm.'

At the hospital, Mrs Wilson and her son, Peter, were
reunited with Gordon and Marie's sister, Julie Anne.
Gordon explained how the wall had fallen on them. Mrs
Wilson remembers: 'I was beginning to get bits of the
story. John Henderson said to me, "The Mullans are
dead." Ronnie Hill was ill.'

While the family waited anxiously for news, surgeons,
nurses and theatre assistants worked to bring Marie's

internal bleeding under control. She had been badly injured in the pelvic area and legs. Blood supply at the hospital was low, but more arrived from Omagh, twenty-six miles away, and she continued to have transfusions. David Bolton continued to search for her:

> She couldn't be found anywhere. She couldn't be found over at the TA Centre, couldn't be found in the hospital mortuary. I went to the wards; she wasn't there. Casualty didn't have her, she wasn't in outpatients. We were getting perturbed and concerned, and then, as a final resort, I decided to go to theatre and knocked on the door.

A member of staff confirmed that they were operating on a young woman. Staff described what she was wearing and gave David a little bracelet, which he brought back to the family. Julie Anne, recognised it at once. Mrs Wilson continues:

> Dr Ritchie, who is the anaesthetist, came in and said he wanted to see the Wilson family, so the curtains were pulled round the bed where Gordon was and he gave us the first news to say that Marie was in theatre and they were fighting for her life. They had given her transfusions, but she was losing blood as fast as they were giving her blood.

Gordon Wilson said to him, 'You are telling us that Marie is dying?' and the doctor replied, 'Well as long as there is life, there is hope, but we are fighting for her life.'

A short time afterwards, another doctor and nurse arrived and brought Mrs Wilson, Peter and Julie Anne into an office. Mrs Wilson remembers:

> The same story — they were fighting for her life, she was badly hurt, her pelvis was broken and she was brain damaged. There was no doubt about that and she was haemorrhaging very heavily. He didn't hold out a lot of hope.

The third call was for the family to come to intensive care. Gordon could not go because of his injuries, but Joan Wilson remembers coming out of the lift:

We met Sister who said 'Now I want to warn you that Marie's heart is only just beating. She is on the machine and her heart may stop at any minute.'

So we were taken into the room and she was lying with many tubes connected to her and her fair hair was very dark. I can always remember that and scratches on her face. The anaesthetist was standing at the bottom of the bed. I went over to her and I touched her and realised she was cold. I stood and kissed her and looked at her. I thought, my goodness, the girl who left this morning full of life, because she whizzed across the yard — now here she was lying just on her last.

When I spoke, I saw her eyelids flicker. I will always see that. Then Sister turned to me and said, 'Her heart has stopped beating.' So the machine was turned off. Well, we just didn't know where to turn, it was just one of those things we will never forget. I turned to leave the room, but I couldn't. I kept coming back to look at her and going out and coming back.

As the mother realised that she had just lost her daughter, she murmured, 'The Lord gave, and the Lord has taken away.'

Then it dawned on her that she would have to go back downstairs to tell her husband. She approached the bed and as Gordon sat up, he asked, 'Well, how is Marie?'

'She is gone.'

'My God, is Marie dead?'

A short time later, the family left the hospital. Methodist minister, the Rev. Tom Magowan, brought Gordon Wilson in a wheelchair out to the car. Mrs Wilson recalls the half-mile journey up to their home at Cooper Crescent:

Peter was driving, Gordon sat in the front, Julie Anne in the back. Gordon said, 'The next few days are going to be very difficult. We will have to muster all the courage and all the strength and dignity we can.' We came home to the house in darkness.

Disbelief

Julian Armstrong was sitting in a cubicle. He was injured, but he knew that his parents were dead. His sister, Stella Robinson, was at home that morning when she heard what she thought was a garage door banging. Then her husband Kenneth's aunt, Angel Robinson, who had tended to Julian at the scene, arrived and spoke to Kenneth.

In the car on the way to the hospital, Stella started to cry and Kenneth warned her, saying, 'Now this mightn't be good. Be prepared.'

Stella replied, 'Maybe they will just be badly injured.'

When they arrived, Stella found Julian straight away and said, 'Julian, tell me where's Mummy and Daddy.'

'They're dead,' Julian told her. 'I know Mummy is dead, but I'm not sure about Daddy. The last time I saw him he shook, his body shook.'

Stella still hoped that her brother might be wrong, and she went around the hospital asking people if they had seen her mother or father. Slowly, the truth sank in, and Methodist ministers held her hand and confirmed it. 'I was just crying and screaming, it was terrible,' she recalls. She then faced the awful task of phoning her sisters, while her husband went down to the TA centre to find the bodies.

Temporary Mortuary

At the temporary mortuary at the other side of town, mutilated bodies were being brought in on old grey canvas stretchers. RUC officers took charge, assisted by members of the Territorial Army. Word had spread that this was where the temporary morgue was, and relatives searching for loved ones were arriving at the gate. An RUC Chief Inspector asked for sheets to cover the bodies hurriedly before relatives came in, but there was no time for undertakers or mortuary assistants to prepare bodies for relatives to see. There are still marks on the floor where the blood would not wash off.

One TA officer, Sam Blair, saw the bodies being

brought in but did not immediately recognise that his wife Ruth's parents, Billy and Nessie Mullan, were among them. Ruth called to say that her parents were missing, and Sam faced the harrowing task of going around the bodies to discover that his parents-in-law were indeed dead. He telephoned the hospital where his brother-in-law, James, was still anxiously looking for them. The other two members of the Mullan family were thousands of miles away: Margaret Veitch was on holiday in Mombasa and Joan Anderson was living in New York.

Tommy Halliwell, his suit and hands still covered in grime, dirt and blood, had walked across town and was now helping at the makeshift morgue. He, like the others, knew most of the victims as they came in:

> We were laying them out and I knew a right few of them. There was another woman — I didn't know her at all. She was from Garvary; she had a lovely necklace on, not a mark on her.

This was Sister Alberta Quinton, a 72-year-old veteran of the Second World War, who was wearing the medals she was awarded in the Women's Royal Air Force. Her son, Derek, had left her off at the War Memorial and was parking his car when the bomb went off. He is clearly seen on the video footage, wandering around, arms open in bewilderment, trying to find his mother. Her whereabouts remained a mystery until someone gave in a handbag at the hospital. It contained her medical card. Derek Quinton was accompanied by a minister when he arrived at the morgue to identify his mother.

The temporary morgue was some distance from a phone, and the site was about a mile from the hospital, so communication was difficult. But information was gradually filtering through.

Scenes at the Erne

Meanwhile, David Bolton continued to help at the Erne hospital:

You kept putting it off and saying the worst couldn't have happened. But as the day went on, first there was six dead, then there was seven, then eight, then nine. The numbers kept building up — this reality was so overwhelming at times. The phone rang and someone would say, 'Hello, this is the BBC newsroom in London.' It just amplified this total sense of drama and unreality. I really thought, why would Enniskillen be going through this? I felt that something awful must have happened in the wider world. It was as if we were a small part of a bigger drama.

In the corridors of the hospital, there were some striking images. Archbishop Robin Eames stood out visually in his bright, clean, purple clerical shirt. He had come with Canon McCarthy, who was hospital chaplain as well as Rector of St Macartin's. Both men were helping to comfort people. Canon McCarthy remembers seeing someone being pushed along on a trolley, 'blood streaming everywhere. But someone was saying, "He's alive." I could just hear the joy in the voice.'

The Roman Catholic parish priest, Monsignor Cahill, was also there, together with Fr Martin Treanor. The Monsignor remembers feeling very tense as many would associate Catholics with the bomb. But he was amazed by the welcome — some people went out of their way to greet him. He spoke to a number of people, among them Harry Donaldson in intensive care

Another churchman present was the Bishop of Clogher, the Right Rev. Brian Hannon, who had informed a shocked congregation in St Macartin's of what had happened.

Bereaved

Gladys Gault was in the congregation at St Macartin's. She had heard the explosion and knew that her husband, Sammy, would be at the parade. He had recently retired because of heart trouble, and as Gladys heard the bang, she thought, 'Gosh, that'll not do Sammy's heart much good.' As the sirens wailed, people were still coming into church and one girl said, 'Something terrible has happened. There has been a bomb and Sammy and Stephen were in it.'

Mrs Gault initially thought that both had been killed: 'I thought I was going to pass out. I got weak and somebody caught me.' She was brought to the hospital .

At first, nobody could tell Gladys Gault for sure that her husband was dead, but her 18-year-old son, Stephen, arrived in an ambulance and gave her the sad news. She did not want to accept it, but he kept saying, 'I'm telling you, I saw him.' Mrs Gault was eventually brought into a side room at the hospital with her friend, Pam Millar, and officially told that her husband had been killed by the bomb.

She returned home to their comfortable bungalow, and as soon as she came through the door the phone started ringing. The first call was from 'Granny Gault', her husband's elderly mother who had heard the news in Larne, Co. Antrim, almost a hundred miles away.

'I want to speak to Sammy. Put Sammy on,' the woman kept saying, until someone broke the news to her, too.

Another woman soon to learn that she had lost her husband was Kathleen Armstrong, who was in the Presbyterian Church Hall, known locally as the Guild Hall. The Rev. David Cupples remembers arriving at the church, which was empty apart from a little group of relatives of a baby about to be christened. They just sat, not knowing what to do. At the back, in the Guild Hall, Rev. Cupples remembers hearing 'wailing':

> I looked around and saw all these people crying and sensed the distress and disturbance in the atmosphere and I began to realise we were dealing with something big, a major tragedy. I remembered a line from a sermon about Jesus stilling the storm on the Sea of Galilee and the preacher said 'Faith is a refusal to panic.' I can remember just standing in the middle of the hall, looking round me. It was a major disaster situation, but that just came into my mind and I thought, 'Right, I am not going to panic.'

The minister was brought immediately to Kathleen Armstrong, who had some minor injuries. He recalls:

> Later in the morning I did actually find her son, Clive, and was able to go and tell Kathleen he was okay. But, of course, Ted was gone.

Mrs Armstrong was brought to the hospital to see Clive, and she was with him when they were told that Ted was killed. 'You are just numb,' she says.

Relatives of the other dead were being sought, too. Johnny Megaw had no family in Enniskillen, but his brother, Bertie, was attending morning service in the Presbyterian church in Ballymena. He had not heard the news that morning and did not know what his minister, the Rev. Russell Birney, meant when he mentioned in prayer the 'catastrophe in Enniskillen'. Some time later he was told that his brother was dead.

Kit and Jessie Johnston's daughter, Ruth Kennedy, was in her home in Ballyclare. She rarely missed church, but had been delayed that morning when she heard that there had been a bomb in Enniskillen. 'I just froze. We just knew that they were there,' says Ruth.

The Media Arrive

While the bereaved were still taking in events, the hospital continued in a flurry of activity. David Bolton was assisting in gathering information, bringing bits of paper down to hospital administrator Norman Hilliard who was trying to deal with a host of enquiries. By half past three in the afternoon, the picture was clearer. We knew who was dead and who was alive. It had been a long day for all the people of Enniskillen.

As massive media operations swung into action, the coming days looked like being tough. The bereaved would have to do their grieving in the glare of publicity; the injured would have to cope with requests for interviews as they tried to deal with the trauma and recover from their injuries.

An American NBC crew was among the first of many newspeople to descend on the quiet little town. The crew members had been working on a story in Dublin in the morning, when they heard the news on radio. They had no idea where Enniskillen was, but asked their taxi driver to bring them there. By afternoon, they were setting up a satellite dish to beam pictures back to the United States.

And then, in the midst of the chaos and the anguish, there was new life: Sara Ternan was born in the Erne hospital on the afternoon of 8 November 1987. Her mother, Jean, had been brought into hospital earlier in the day for a Caesarean Section, but had to wait while staff dealt with the emergency. By four o'clock she could wait no longer and was wheeled into the operating theatre, which staff had no time to clear up. Sara, weighing 8 pounds 10 ounces, was delivered in a theatre surrounded by the debris of earlier efforts to save lives. Her parents, Jean and Bill, found it difficult to express their joy.

3: Salt of the Earth

> I always said that Satan caused the bomb, but the Lord chose the people.

These are the words of Noreen Hill, whose husband Ronnie has been in a coma since two days after the Enniskillen bomb. For ten years, Noreen has not only shown total devotion in looking after her husband, but has also demonstrated remarkable and unshakeable Christian faith. She is quick to recognise the goodness in others and feels that God selected those who died because they were 'ready to go', by which she means that they were Christians who were prepared to die and meet their maker.

News spreads rapidly around a small town. By the time the names of the eleven victims were officially released to the media on the Sunday evening of the tragedy, most of the local community already knew who they were:

Billy Mullan (74), and his wife, Nessie (73)
Wesley Armstrong (62), and his wife, Bertha (55)
Kit Johnston (71), and his wife, Jessie (62)
Alberta Quinton (72)
Johnny Megaw (67)
Ted Armstrong (52)
Sammy Gault (49)
and the youngest, 20-year-old Marie Wilson.

To the outside world, these were eleven names, but to the people of Enniskillen they were their neighbours — 'the salt of the earth'.

Six of the dead were members of the Presbyterian Church, three were Methodists and two were Church of Ireland. As time went on, people were struck by the fact that despite many different characteristics, the eleven victims had so much in common. Many were involved in caring professions such as helping the sick, and every single one was a genuinely religious person, a regular churchgoer whose Christian faith was not just a label, but a large part of their life.

Johnny Megaw

Johnny Megaw, a 67-year-old retired painter, lived alone in Derrin Road in Enniskillen. A jovial man who cycled everywhere, he was a familiar figure around the town, not least because every Saturday he would stand at the Diamond — an area of pavement in the town centre — preaching with a small group of born-again Christians. The day before the bombing, Johnny was taking part in the little open-air meeting as usual when he encountered some heckling from a passer-by who accused him of talking rubbish, and asked, 'Where would you be if you died in the morning?'

Johnny replied, 'My body would be buried and my soul would go to be with Christ, my Saviour.' In the morning, Johnny Megaw was dead, killed instantly when the bombed building fell on him. The Saturday meeting he had attended was one he had been supporting for over forty years.

Johnny Megaw was born in the tiny village of Maboy, near Portglenone in Co. Antrim. His mother died when he was just two-and-a-half, leaving him and a little six-month-old baby brother. Their father later remarried, moved away, and had little contact with the boys who were brought up by their grandmother. When she died, Johnny was just 14, and his father sent him as an apprentice to a Mr Myers in Larne.

Johnny often told Saturday-morning shoppers and passers-by, as well as people at numerous other gospel meetings, how he had been 'saved' as a 14-year-old, and had followed a Christian life ever since. On Friday, 15 February 1933, he had gone with his uncle to a gospel mission in a hall in Larne to hear a Mr Tom Ray preach. The message had touched him and he had 'invited Jesus Christ to come into my heart and life as my personal Saviour'. He would always implore people: 'Friend, if you are not yet born again, no matter what your past is, the Saviour is seeking you.'

In 1941, his apprenticeship served, Johnny was sent by his new boss on contracts to Enniskillen to paint war huts. It was at this time that he was introduced to a group of evangelical Christians there. He moved to live in the town in 1952 although he had no family there, and became involved with the born-again Christians' open-air meetings at the Diamond where they would sing hymns and preach. They also undertook visits to local hospitals, and Johnny became a familiar figure there every Sunday. At Christmas he would spend most of his meagre earnings buying gifts for the sick and elderly. After his death, a portrait of Johnny was commissioned, and it now hangs in the geriatric wing of the Erne hospital.

Following the bombing, Bertie Megaw travelled to Enniskillen to carry out the necessary arrangements to fulfil his brother's wish of being buried in a family plot back in Ballymena, where he was known as Jack.

Over a hundred of Johnny's Christian friends gathered in silent tribute as his remains left the town where he had made his home and been so cruelly cut down. They sang hymns and accompanied the hearse out of Enniskillen. One of them, a local businessman, later wrote to Mr Megaw's brother, criticising him for not having Johnny buried in Enniskillen.

'I felt cut up with that,' says Bertie Megaw. 'I didn't know the score down in Enniskillen. My brother made his own arrangements for the grave.'

In addition to the honour from his evangelical Christian friends, there were tributes from all types of people in Fermanagh, including the Catholic Church. Bertie Megaw received a touching letter from a Roman Catholic nun, and in the week after the bomb, Fr Brian D'Arcy spoke fondly of Johnny Megaw on RTÉ's *Late Late Show*, recalling his own schooldays in Enniskillen when he would hear Johnny preaching about the love of God.

Sister Alberta Quinton

Alberta Coulter came from of a family of eleven children in Inver, Co. Donegal. One of the three Ulster counties in the Republic, Donegal continued to have large pockets of Protestant communities after partition. Having trained in England, Alberta joined the Women's Royal Air Force nursing section and saw service in the Second World War in North Africa, Italy and Yugoslavia. She could often be persuaded to relate stories from this interesting chapter of her life, such as the audience she had with Pope Pius XII when stationed in Rome. His Holiness had seen the group of WRAF women and asked to meet them, making Alberta the envy of one of her four close friends — the only Catholic among them was unable to be with her comrades that particular day.

Her daughter, Aileen, recalls:

> She was great fun. Her faith meant a lot to her, but apart from that her main philosophy in life would have been to help other people whenever and however you can; and enjoy yourself and have lots of fun.

After the war, Alberta had a couple of job offers including one at Enniskillen and one at Singapore. She chose Enniskillen and went there in 1950, becoming a much-loved character in both the old Erne hospital and the county hospital. She married local government officer George Quinton who was also in the RAF, but was stationed in his native Fermanagh and in England. They met at a dance in the nurses' home. Aileen says:

> I think she had been to lots and lots of dances as well as working hard. Any time some old RAF boy was on *This is*

Your Life, we'd say, 'Well, did you dance with him?' It would be 'Oh yes.'

George and Alberta Quinton brought up their three sons, Derek, Christopher and Ian, and daughter, Aileen, at his family home at Killyvilly. Three years before the Enniskillen bomb, George Quinton died of Alzheimer's Disease. Alberta had shown great devotion in looking after her husband through his illness.

Seventy-two-year-old Sister Quinton had had a long career in nursing and was described once as 'the sort of person who could make things all right by simply being there'. She had many fine qualities, being practical and down to earth, as well as a mother figure to patients and young nursing staff. A car accident had left her with one leg slightly shorter than the other, but this never prevented her from enjoying life to the full.

Being at the War Memorial was important to her. She never missed the Remembrance Sunday ceremony, when she could pay homage to colleagues in the Air Force who had been shot down and killed in the War, explaining that during the War there had been no time to grieve:

> We would read the name on the notice board and go into the Mess. You would have a drink to their memory and that would be it; you wouldn't mention them again because there was too much to be done.

Every year, the night before Remembrance Sunday, she would take out her medals and give them a polish. On the morning of her death, her main concern was remembering which was the correct side to wear the medals on. She followed her usual ritual of leaving her prayer book sitting out at home; after the Remembrance ceremony she intended to call in to collect it, have a quick cup of tea and go on to noon service at Garvary Church of Ireland Parish Church. The prayer book was never collected.

Every year Alberta Quinton would stand at the same place for the ceremony. In 1986, however, she had been thoroughly soaked and remembered having seen someone cleverly sheltering in a phone box. In 1987, Alberta Quinton decided to leave the position she normally took up and go over to the Reading Rooms wall.

Kit and Jessie Johnston

Among the eleven people killed were three married couples. Standing close to Sister Quinton were Kit and Jessie Johnston, who had both served the community of Fermanagh at the Erne hospital — Kit as an ambulance driver and Jessie as a nurse.

Richard Kitchener Johnston, or Kit as he came to be known, was born at Cherrymount, Enniskillen. He was named after the famous First World War leader General Kitchener. His twin brother was named Robert French Johnston after General French. There were three sets of twins in the family of eight, but Kit was generally regarded fondly as 'the ringleader'.

Kit was a well-known figure at the hospital where he worked for twenty-nine years until his retirement in 1981. He was awarded the British Empire Medal in the Honours list, for his service to the community.

While helping the sick and injured in the 1950s, romance blossomed at the hospital when he met a young nurse, Jessie McKinley, from Kesh, Co. Fermanagh. A nurse at the former Fermanagh County Hospital, and at the Erne hospital from 1955 until her retirement in 1986, Jessie proved the perfect partner, sharing not only similar work but also common interests such as gardening. According to their daughter, Ruth Kennedy:

> They worked hard all their life; they would always do a good turn for people and were always on the go. There was nobody like them. Yet they were robbed of their retirement.

Ruth herself was just a toddler when her father joined the ambulance service in 1952 at the Erne hospital. After the departure of his first wife, there was a strong bond between father and daughter, and in those days he would often bundle up the infant in his arms and take her with him on ambulance runs.

Jessie, who was 62 when she was killed, loved her nursing work. 'She was the best in the world,' says Ruth. 'Anybody with any need, they were there.' Jessie would always go out into the garden before Remembrance Sunday and get some foliage just to dress up their poppies a little. She was a quiet-natured woman who played the piano and taught her grand-daughter, Sharon, to draw.

Mr and Mrs Johnston were very private people, completely at ease enjoying their family. A 71-year-old grandfather, Kit Johnston loved nothing more than playing in the garden with his grandchildren near his home at Drumgay just beside a wildlife reserve outside Enniskillen. 'He was just a big child himself,' recalls Ruth, who treasures lovely memories of her son Richard (then 12) and 8-year-old Sharon having great times with their grandad and granny.

Ruth and Joe Kennedy and their children lived at Ballyclare, Co. Antrim, and the families would take it in turns every other Sunday to undertake the two-hour journey to visit each other; the first thing they would do on arrival home was to phone to say that they had got back safely.

Kit Johnston's two sons, Desmond and David, and other daughter, Irene, were living in Swindon in England when he died. They faced a sad journey home for the double funeral in Enniskillen Presbyterian church. It was the first funeral ever attended by Ruth, then in her thirties.

At the funeral, her husband, Joe Kennedy, read from 1 Cor 13, a passage based on Christian love and charity. 'I felt it was relevant to them and their lives, which transcended all the bitterness and hate,' he said.

Wesley and Bertha Armstrong

Sixty-two-year-old Wesley Armstrong died along with his wife, Bertha. Good church-going folk, in many ways they were a typical rural Fermanagh Protestant married couple. He was the strict, yet loving, father who spent much of his life at church activities, she the devoted wife and mother who combined keeping the home together with sometimes working part-time to help provide for the family.

Wesley Armstrong was born near Maguiresbridge, eight miles from Enniskillen. In 1954, he married Bertha Houston whom he met when they both worked at the Scotch Store bacon factory in Enniskillen. Aged 55 when she was killed, she was from the country area of Springfield and in the early years the couple lived in rural Fermanagh; in Cavancarragh and then Lisnaan, ending up in Chanterhill, a housing estate on the outskirts of Enniskillen.

Wesley was Superintendent of the Methodist Sunday School in Enniskillen and a circuit steward in the church. When his three daughters were children they would be brought to church three times on a Sunday: Lisbellaw in the morning, Maguiresbridge in the afternoon, and back to Lisbellaw for evening service.

A lover of music, he was also in the church choir. His favourite hymn was 'Thine Be The Glory', and he was proud that his Christian name was famously Methodist. He also loved to sing solos at family weddings, and used to play the trumpet in Maguiresbridge Silver Band. The bands playing in the Remembrance Sunday parade were one of the attractions of the occasion for him.

Wesley Armstrong worked for eight years for British Telecom after a long career with Customs and Excise. His work as a 'customs man' had brought him into contact with many people throughout Fermanagh and across the Border. After his death, among the many letters received by his family were a large number from the Republic and from Catholic families in Northern Ireland.

Bertha Armstrong loved the country life. She kept a few cows and ducks, and people would call to buy the eggs that her hens produced. She had pet names for all the hens. And she baked bread and cake for the family. Her oldest daughter, Stella Robinson, remembers:

The week before she was killed she mentioned to me that we should never have moved from the country. She said that was where she was the happiest.

Stella also remembers getting porridge for breakfast 'whether you liked it or not!' She has many special memories of her parents:

> Mummy and Daddy would always have called round on a Sunday when my husband, Kenneth, was working. My youngest brother, Julian, would come with them and they would collect me and my kids. We would all go for a family walk around Florence Court or Castle Archdale, or even down south to Rossnowlagh or Bundoran in Co. Donegal.

The summer before the bomb, Stella's father-in-law died, and as Kenneth was coming to terms with the loss the couple took a few days' break on their own, with Wesley and Bertha looking after their three children.

> It was wonderful for them because my daughter, Janice, stayed in their room. Mummy would come in and Daddy would have the Bible out and Janice sitting up beside him reading it. I thought it was a lovely memory. Janice is engaged now — they would have been so proud.

Family was important to Wesley and Bertha Armstrong. In addition to Stella, they had two other daughters, Pam and Moyna, whom the couple had visited in England — the first time they had been on a plane. Their two sons still lived at home: Trevor and 16-year-old Julian, who was standing between his parents when they died. Julian remembers playing football and tennis with his father:

> Even though he was over 60 he could still give me a run for my money. I was close to him, but I think closer to my mum. He was a strict Methodist, no TV on a Sunday. He was strict with my sisters and brother, but I think he mellowed a bit when I came along.
>
> My mother was a loving, caring woman. She worked her hands to the bone for us, for the family. She was a laugh though. People said she was quiet, but at home I think she was actually louder than Dad.

William and Nessie Mullan

Like the other two married couples, William and Nessie Mullan's lives centred around their home and family, their work and their church. Neither was originally from Fermanagh, but they met when their work brought them to Enniskillen, and they lived there for half a century.

Agnes Mann, known as Nessie, was from a farming background in Armagh. As a young woman, she moved to Enniskillen in the 1930s to work in the ladies fashion department of Harron's drapery in High Street, the shop later taken over by Gordon Wilson's father. In nearby Townhall Street, her husband to be, William Mullan, originally from Limavady in Co. Derry, was managing Stephenson's Pharmacy. As a young man, William was an accomplished golfer and cricketer, and he played Rugby, but he stopped playing when the family came along.

The Mullans lived on Enniskillen's Sligo Road for over twenty years, and it remained home for their three daughters, Margaret, Ruth and Joan, and only son, James, even after they had grown up and married. Their eldest daughter, Margaret Veitch, remembers her mother:

> She was the greatest soother. When I was worried or annoyed, Mummy would put her arm around me. She was a very touchy person and always had a lovely smile.

The couple worked hard all their lives. William Mullan built up a successful pharmacy of his own in Darling Street, which became something of an institution in the town. His wife was a real 'homemaker'. A member of the Women's Institute, she loved working in her garden, and her family enjoyed her home baking. She would always bake extra and have plenty for her family to bring away with them when they called.

Both Nessie and Billy Mullan were great supporters of the church. Nessie was a member of the Presbyterian choir in Enniskillen, while Billy Mullan was an elder in the church and had been the Sunday School Superintendent for over twenty years.

James Mullan became a pharmacist and worked in the business alongside his father for over twenty years. He remembers his father as a meticulous man, in business and in life. He also recalls his pride in his ancestry:

> He was very proud of his traditions. The Mullan clan from north Derry were not Scottish settlers — we are Celtic Irish and can trace our family history right back. That was something he was very proud of. It was very important that Mullan was spelt with an 'a' and he would often send letters back.

Being in business in Northern Ireland throughout the Troubles was difficult, and William Mullan would often have to come into the shop at night to check for incendiary or fire-bomb devices. He was a quiet, yet determined man and hated to see property being destroyed. James explains:

> That just went against his grain completely. One worked hard, one had respect for the other community, you paid your taxes and whatever you earned you could spend whatever way you wanted. To see property being destroyed was something he couldn't understand.

Away from business, the Mullans enjoyed a happy family life. In summer they would often pack up the car on a Sunday and head for Portnoo in Co. Donegal for a picnic. They worked together on the garden — he would do the physical work, digging and cutting the grass, while her green fingers would tend the shrubs. They did everything together.

William and Nessie Mullan were taken together on a November morning in 1987. At the time of their deaths, William was 74, Nessie 73.

Sammy Gault

Two of the dead served in the RUC. Forty-nine-year-old Sammy Gault had been a sergeant but had retired in 1983, having suffered a heart attack the previous year.

His death on Remembrance Sunday 1987 was a cruel irony: he had survived an IRA attack exactly twenty-six years earlier. In 1961, also on Remembrance Sunday, he was part of an RUC patrol in Jonesborough in south Armagh, when the IRA opened fire from behind a church wall. A colleague, Willie Hunter, was killed, and Sammy Gault was shot in the leg. The bullet went through the old-style long police coat and lodged in his knee.

The young constable, originally from Larne, Co. Antrim, was then in his third year in the RUC. After six months' injury leave, he continued with his lengthy police career.

While in the RUC training depot in 1958, Sammy had met local girl Gladys Clarke. They married in 1960, and together moved around Northern Ireland. Sammy served in Dromara, Co. Down; Forkhill, Co. Armagh; Ballina-mallard and Irvinestown, Co. Fermanagh, and Glengorm-ley, Belfast. As the Troubles were starting in the late 1960s, the couple moved to Omagh where Sammy became a sergeant. He later became the first training officer in Fermanagh for the newly formed RUC Reserve, and this allowed them to move back to Gladys's native county.

The couple had two sons: 18-year-old Stephen was standing beside his father when the bomb went off. His older brother, Keith, was on his way over the nearby east bridge, delayed as people stopped him to admire his baby boy, Andrew, in his pushchair.

Sammy was dedicated to his career, but time at home was always precious. He was close to his sons and devoted to his new grandson. His retirement meant that he could collect Andrew every morning and bring him to the lovely bungalow at Benaughlin Park, where he and Gladys lived. The couple enjoyed gardening together, and she points to the tall Canadian poplar trees out the back and remembers the day he planted them: 'He said, "These will be for the grandchildren to climb."'

After his retirement, Sammy joined Gladys as a member of the Red Cross, and together they helped to deliver meals on wheels to the elderly. Both were 'born-again'

Christians and attended the Rev. Ian Paisley's Free Presbyterian church. Gladys explains:

> We both got saved at a gospel mission in Lisbellaw in the 1970s. Sammy had a very strong faith. It helped me to deal with things when I knew he was saved.

After his death, Gladys discovered that Sammy had marked a passage in his Bible from the book of Proverbs:

> These . . . things doth the Lord hate . . . hands that shed innocent blood (Proverbs 6: 16–17).

Ted Armstrong

The second policeman to die had also been 'saved' a few years before his death. Edward McMorris Armstrong, known as Ted, was 52 and from Brookeborough, Co. Fermanagh. He had served in the 'B' Specials, the RUC's part-time auxiliary which was disbanded in the early 1970s. He then went into the RUC Reserve, and was in the RUC station in Enniskillen in 1985 when mortar bombs rocketed down on it.

His wife, Kathleen, recalls: 'That bomb had a big effect on him. He took into reading his Bible a lot.'

At his funeral in Enniskillen Presbyterian church, the Rev. John Faris read out notes found in Ted Armstrong's Bible:

> Rocket attack on RUC depot. God's miracle, 16 rockets but nobody killed. Got very ill, nervous tension and headaches, crying etc.

> September 25th, 2.30 a.m. asked for God's help. Asked him to come into my life as my Saviour and Friend and to forgive me my sins. God did and has been my friend ever since. Something really happened to me that night. I became a new person filled with the Holy Spirit.

Ted's 16-year-old son, Clive, was injured in the bomb and attended the funeral on crutches.

Ted and Kathleen were married in 1958. Together with Clive they were a close-knit family. A well-known angler,

Ted loved the Fermanagh lakes and would often bring his catch of fish home to the neighbours and family. He had his own boat and enjoyed bringing members of the Disabled Police Officers' Association out on trips. Kathleen recalls:

> He was very good to the elderly. He wouldn't do anybody any harm. He was a giver. But they were all really good people who died. They all served the community in one way or another: Mr and Mrs Mullan, Mr and Mrs Johnston — you could not have nicer people. Mrs Mullan was a terrific woman, she had only to put her arm round you and was a great comfort. Johnny Megaw would have given everything.

Ted Armstrong was always conscious of the precarious nature of his career, particularly during the several years he acted as driver and bodyguard for former Ulster Unionist leader, Mr Harry West. He once told his wife that if anything happened, he would 'like to go quick'.

He could not have expected to die while standing with other civilians at a ceremony to pay homage to the dead.

Marie Wilson

Much has been said and written about Marie Wilson, partly because of the extraordinary interview given by her father, Gordon Wilson, when he said that he would pray for her killers, and partly because, at 20, she was by far the youngest victim.

According to her former career guidance teacher, Kate Doherty:

> There was nothing about Marie that I felt anyone exaggerated in any of the things written. She really was a very fine girl.

Miss Doherty knew Marie from her days as deputy head girl at the Collegiate Girls' Grammar School, and says:

> She was a lovely girl. She was very plain spoken, in one sense straightforward, no nonsense and practical. But with a great charm as well, a really nice girl.

Tall and striking in appearance, Marie was the youngest of the family, with an older brother, Peter, and sister, Julie Ann. She was about to start her third year as a student nurse at the Royal Victoria Hospital in Belfast. Like her mother, Joan, who taught her to play the violin, she loved music. She was in the nurses' choir, taking part in concerts and entertaining the patients. Joan remembers her energy:

> She rushed about and she loved people. She loved activity: tennis, swimming and gymnastics; she just kept going all the time. When she came home, she would just take over the kitchen and I still miss all that now; she was full of cheer.

Marie lived life to the full. The summer before she died she spent a three-week cycling holiday in the Netherlands.

Joan says that father and daughter had a special bond. In interviews after she was killed, he referred to her as 'the pet'. Joan says:

> Gordon loved all of them equally but she was the youngest and they got on very well together. He disciplined her but there was a great bond. They seemed to have the same sense of humour. I think he was very pleased she did nursing because his mother had been a Royal-trained nurse and he had a great bond with his mother.

Gordon used to worry about his daughter living and working in trouble-torn Belfast. Ironically, it was when she was home in Enniskillen that her life was taken. Joan says:

> I am glad I had her so long and the memories are just lovely. As her father said, she is in a better place and we will meet again.

A Town's Loss

For a town like Enniskillen, to lose eleven people in one incident like this was bound to be traumatic. Clearly, in addition to the very nature of the tragedy, the kind of people who died had a profound impact on the small

community. Townspeople felt genuine affection for those
who died.

David Bolton, a social worker who worked closely with
the bereaved in the years following the bomb, says:

> Some people saw what happened as something apocalyp-
> tic; that eleven good people were taken as some sort of
> sign or judgment by God on the people of Northern Ire-
> land. It was a sacrifice and that was woven into people's
> religious response. Not everybody felt that but some peo-
> ple felt that. It was quite strong. I heard it said on a
> number of occasions, that eleven good people were taken;
> they were the salt of the earth, they were all lovely people
> and that is how people reach the conclusion.

However, as a practising Christian, David Bolton himself
would not agree with this Old Testament idea of sacrifice:

> I don't think God ever imposes suffering on us. I do be-
> lieve that God is able to use the circumstances we find
> ourselves in to demonstrate that love will triumph over
> evil. I think suffering is part of the condition that we live
> with as human beings — as one of my favourite writers
> says, it is the mechanical necessity of life.

Enniskillen architect Richard Pierce was involved in the
subsequent work to redesign the War Memorial to incor-
porate the names of those who died. In correspondence
he made the point that 'part of the pathos of the situation
is in the modesty of those who died.'

4: A Town in Mourning

Ireland's past is littered with tragedy. In the past thirty years in particular, Northern Ireland has seen thousands of killings. These include many incidents of horrible multiple deaths as a result of actions by both Republican and Loyalist paramilitaries, and also people killed by the security forces. Yet no single incident unleashed such a massive outpouring of public sympathy from around the world as the Enniskillen bombing.

Journalists from many international organisations arrived and in the next few days messages of sympathy and support poured in from all corners of Ireland and Britain, and from countries as diverse as Pakistan and Canada.

Though Enniskillen was later to become a symbol of hope, in the days following the tragedy it was a symbol of agony. Many of the images were simple, yet powerful. On the Sunday evening, the scheduled service at Enniskillen Presbyterian church went ahead. Rev. David Cupples had been minister for just eight weeks. The television cameras were allowed into the church to film him breaking the news to his congregation that six of their members had been killed.

'We've lost Billy and Nessie Mullan, Kit and . . .' he began, before breaking down momentarily. He explains:

> Strangely enough I hadn't felt emotion all day; I think your mind was numbed. But the quiet dignity and formality of the church service just brought the first flood of emotion to the surface.

The entire town of 15,000 went into mourning for four days of funerals. Social worker David Bolton recalls:

> Thousands of people attended and walked in silence after the hearses as they moved through the town to the graveyards. It was here that the sorrow and outrage of the community was seen and expressed. This was a community in grief. Its tears were on the solemn faces of its people.

Enniskillen awoke on Monday morning, its residents not knowing what had hit their town. A few shops remained open for the basics: milk, bread and newspapers. Almost everywhere else closed. David Bolton remembers walking through the town on the Monday morning:

> It was just unbelievable. It was like a ghost town. The town itself just seemed to speak, the buildings, the absence of people.

Gordon Wilson Interview

It was in this atmosphere of raw poignancy that the now-famous interview with Gordon Wilson was broadcast. Having being told at the Erne hospital that his daughter had died, Mr Wilson went home with the remaining members of his family. His wife, Joan, recalls that he was very strong; he had 'gathered himself' although in pain.

On the Sunday evening, two representatives of the BBC arrived. Charlie Warmington, a producer with the BBC in Belfast, was an Enniskillen man and knew the Wilsons well. He was accompanied by reporter Mike Gaston. Mrs Wilson says:

> I was so busy with people and answering phones that I didn't know Gordon was giving an interview. He just told his story simply. I know from previous times seeing him watch people who had lost relatives that he always dreaded them saying something that would incite the situation.

She says that Gordon Wilson did not realise the impact his words would have. He told Mike Gaston of his recollection of the bomb going off. He was buried under rubble, and then somebody grabbed his hand:

> It was Marie. Marie said, 'Is that you, Daddy?'
> I said, 'Yes.'
> 'Are you all right, Daddy?' she asked.
> I said, 'I'm fine.'
> Three or four times I asked her if she was all right and each time she replied, 'I'm fine, how are you?' I said, 'Hold on. They will be coming to have us out soon.'
> Then she said, 'Daddy, I love you very much.' That was the last thing she said.
> I have lost my daughter, and we shall miss her. But I bear no ill will, I bear no grudge. Dirty sort of talk is not going to bring her back to life. She was a great wee lassie. She was a pet and she's dead. She's in Heaven and we'll meet again. Don't ask me, please, for a purpose. I don't have an answer. But I know there has to be a plan . . . it's part of a greater plan, and God is good. And we shall meet again.

Gerry Burns, then Clerk and Chief Executive of Fermanagh District Council, describes the interview as a 'world stopper'. David Bolton agrees, saying that it was 'deeply moving and powerful':

> Looked at outside Enniskillen it was an incredible contrast, very much turning the other cheek. It was a very powerful symbolic event.

Many people still recall being reduced to tears by it. However, the interview and Gordon Wilson's later role caused some resentment among some families and townspeople, who felt that he was used by the media and that they had been forgotten. But they realise that at the time it cushioned others from attention.

Most other families felt unable or unwilling to give interviews. James Mullan arrived back at his home on Sunday evening, having lost his father and mother:

> I have a large area of tarmac at the front of the house and there were several newspaper and television people inside the gate. My solicitor who is also a friend, Raymond

Ferguson, asked me what I wanted to do. I said, 'This is crazy, Raymond.' They were now in the house and I said, 'Get them out.' It was neither the time or place to start giving interviews.

A week later, on the following Sunday, James Mullan felt able to be interviewed by journalist Brendan Wright on RTÉ radio, when he expressed the hope that something good would come out of the disaster.

Most of the families had minimal dealings with the hordes of press who had arrived in the town. They gave out photos and details of the dead through friends or other members of the family. What they were more concerned with immediately was not only coming to terms with such a violent and sudden loss of a loved one, but having to hold their funeral in the full glare of publicity.

The Funerals

The funerals were massive events. They began at midday on Tuesday when a service for Marie Wilson was held in the Methodist church, while at the same time a service was being held for Ted Armstrong at the Presbyterian church. Both churches were packed and loudspeakers were set up outside where many townspeople stood around the streets listening in silence. Marie Wilson's cortège left the Methodist church, and its route to the town's Breandrum Cemetery took it past the Presbyterian church where Ted Armstrong's funeral was still in progress. For a few moments the two funerals merged, with the loudspeaker relaying the sermon by the Presbyterian minister being switched off briefly to allow the other funeral to pass in silence.

David Bolton was one of those in charge of arrangements at the door of the church for Marie's funeral:

Firstly we had to manage the media; I remember we had German and French crews, Americans, BBC, ITN and RTÉ. I remember the politician Austin Currie coming up to the door and by that time we literally couldn't get another person into the church. He stood outside with so many others who were weeping.

Ted Armstrong was given an RUC burial. The Chief Constable, Sir John Hermon, was among the mourners, and the coffin was draped with the Union flag, with the dead man's police cap on top. The service was also attended by Alderman Tim Leddin, Mayor of Limerick, in his mayoral robes, one of many displays of solidarity in sympathy from the Republic.

In the afternoon, a service was held for Sammy Gault in St Macartin's Church of Ireland cathedral. The Bishop of Clogher, the Right Rev. Brian Hannon, expressed the hope that this would mark a turning point in history:

> This could be the crossroads in our years of communal strife, the week when we made the conscious decision to create a future together rather than to let any element in our society divide and destroy us.

More of the funerals took place on the Wednesday. At the Methodist church, the coffins of Wesley and Bertha Armstrong sat side by side at the front as their three daughters and two sons comforted each other.

At the Presbyterian church, there was another double funeral — that of Kit and Jessie Johnston. The Rev. James Hughes referred to the day as 'Enniskillen's blackest'. Like a number of the other funerals, the Johnston procession passed the tangled remains of the devastated Reading Rooms building.

A couple of miles outside the town, at Garvary parish church, the funeral took place of Alberta Quinton. It was not covered by the BBC, a fact which caused additional distress to the family. Her daughter, Aileen, explains that it was as if this old woman did not really matter — yet she had lived such a wonderful life and contributed so much to the community, and this mattered to the many who knew her.

Also on Wednesday, Johnny Megaw was being buried

in his native Ballymena, eighty miles away, where the Rev. Russell Birney said:

> Johnny's death will not have been in vain if it makes Christian people see that the real enemy is not even those pathetic killers enslaved as they are by hatred and bitterness, but Satan himself.

The last funeral service took place on Thursday, again in the Presbyterian church, this time for Billy and Nessie Mullan. The wind and rain howled down East Bridge Street. Mr and Mrs Mullan's daughter, Margaret Veitch, remembers seeing the two coffins, each with a single red rose on top:

> To see one coffin coming out of the church was bad enough; then I saw the second one coming out. Somehow, you get the strength to cope. We were crushing and breaking inside; my cousin told me and my two sisters to hold our heads up.
>
> I remember coming out of the church to the most awful silence from a sea of faces. A woman who had driven up from Cork came forward and said, 'I had to be with you today,' and shook our hands. We shook hands with people until our hands were numb.

Thousands of Protestants and Catholics attended the funerals in a show of solidarity in adversity. Attendance at funerals is important in rural Irish culture. Usually when mourners follow the coffins of friends or neighbours there is a murmur of conversation. But David Bolton remembers:

> There was a tremendous silence about these funerals. The silence was stunning, particularly as we walked past the cenotaph. There were so many people there that most of us never got near the graveside.

Suffer Little Children

Among those who stood in reverent silence were hundreds of local schoolchildren in their uniforms. Many had been at the scene of the bombing and had connections with the victims. Mrs Toni Johnson, art teacher at Enniskillen High School, has since worked closely with many of the pupils affected by events. She has clear memories of the scenes on the Monday morning after the bomb:

> The school opened at the usual time. There was a very high turnout of pupils and a full turnout of staff, except for our principal who was badly injured and had been admitted to Altnagelvin hospital. Our senior master, Graham Ross, was also absent because his son, Stephen, had been injured and had been taken to Derry by helicopter.
>
> The children were very quiet. They stood in silence in the assembly hall, waiting. The vice-principal went up to the stage and without preamble told the pupils exactly what the situation was.
>
> Mr Hill and Stephen Ross were critically injured and in Altnagelvin hospital. Ian Carson had severe leg injuries. Clive Armstrong was in hospital with leg injuries, having lost his father. Serena Dixon, our head girl, was up at hospital with her critically ill father.

Mrs Johnson continues:

> We said a prayer. Children were crying. We put in the day. Each class was quietly restrained. No one knew what to do or what to say to the children. They worked quietly.
>
> At break time I was on duty in the hall. I think it was then that the full horror hit me. There were children on crutches and with bandaged heads; children with elastoplast on cuts. There were a lot of injured children who had actually come to school, which was quite strange. One girl wore a surgical collar, another had a bruised face. I think that they probably came to school because it was somewhere they knew was all right.

Mrs Johnson recalls going down to one class of fifth years in which four pupils had been to see their friend, Clive Armstrong, in hospital. Mrs Johnson recalls:

> One of the girls was crying. They went very quiet and turned round to look at me as if they expected I could do

something wise that would make things all right. But I couldn't.

Television cameras and reporters arrived at the school gate but were asked to leave.

Later, Mrs Johnson would become involved in helping the children to pick up the threads of their lives, but in the first few days it was a case of getting through the funerals:

> The children all went in uniform and they were very quiet and very reverent. You felt very proud of them really. The ones that were there on the morning were probably still in some sort of shock, but despite the media attention none of them reacted badly.

Across town, the staff and pupils at the Collegiate Grammar School were coming to terms with the fact that their former deputy head girl, Marie Wilson, was one of the eleven people killed. Kate Doherty, now principal and then careers teacher, recalls the atmosphere in the staffroom on the Monday morning. One teacher had not known that Marie was among the victims. She burst into tears and was comforted by colleagues. Another teacher had been in the Erne hospital visiting her sick mother on Sunday and was reliving her experience of being caught up in the confusion of a disaster. Miss Doherty remembers:

> When the bell rang this group of staff moved out to meet their classes. The corridors seemed eerily quiet although there were groups of pupils everywhere. I came down the corridor a bit later to my sixth-form class. Normally you would hear them before you got to the room, a group of sixth formers chatting about the weekend. But there was just this silence. They just looked up in silence, looked at me in a sort of look which said, 'Tell us it is not true' or 'Can you do something about this?'
>
> I think I would honestly say that it was one of the most inadequate moments in one's life. Some were weeping quietly, others comforting them, while the rest sat looking sad and bemused. I stumbled out a few words, then went around hearing their stories of being at the

cenotaph, knowing those killed or injured, and trying to comfort as best I could.

Miss Doherty and the principal, George Young, discussed how they should approach school assembly scheduled for later in the morning. They were worried about creating an emotional atmosphere which would cause even more distress:

> I remember going to a colleague, John Henderson, and talking to him. I felt, I suppose, as a Christian, that surely there must be something that could be said that could be a comfort. If one's faith meant anything, surely it had to mean something at a time like this. We read what we thought were words of comfort from the Bible and we prayed for the people who had been bereaved and injured.

Many of the pupils in the all-girls school cried in the assembly hall and teachers moved through the room comforting them.

> I just remember it being a day that was like as long as a week really. You thought you were never going to get to the end of it. You did everything just moment by moment; day by day you just reacted.

Other schools, such as Portora Royal School and the Enniskillen Model Primary School had similar experiences. At Portora, the school's annual ceremony in remembrance of former pupils who died in wars was attended by the principal of St Michael's College, the Rev. Macartan McQuaid and six pupils.

The Catholic Community

Education in Northern Ireland is segregated. Most Protestants go to state schools, known as 'controlled' schools, while the Roman Catholic Church has a significant input into the ethos of 'maintained' schools. Generally, everyone recognises them as Protestant and Catholic schools. Because Remembrance Sunday is associated with the

Protestant community, the Catholic schools in the town were not directly affected. However, there was a feeling of solidarity from them.

Sister Ann Marie, principal at St Fanchea's school, explains that her students had previously worked on joint projects with Enniskillen High School, and there are strong links between all schools in the town:

> All the Catholic schools closed that week so that we could be present at the funeral services. We were a whole community shocked and grieving. I found a bonding afterwards. In our school, we were grieving for the suffering of the people and that is what I sensed in the whole Catholic community, just a grief and disbelief.

The parish priest in Enniskillen, Monsignor Seán Cahill, says that members of the Catholic community were 'stunned and overwhelmed'. He continues:

> There was a sense of guilt attached to us and we had to convince our Protestant neighbours that we didn't want this. Actually I will never forget it. People were ringing me up, people from our own congregation, in tears, saying 'Why has it come to this? Why has this happened?' There was a sense of frustration, a sense of total hopelessness and, indeed, a sense of fear; like, what is going to happen now?

On Monday morning, those turning up for ten o'clock Mass at St Michael's church were approached by reporters and asked for their opinions. Monsignor Cahill recalls:

> Suddenly they found that the whole attention of the world was on them and they were frightened and disturbed and fearful. It seemed that the bomb had come from our side — therefore I knew that my own position was very difficult. It was very sensitive.

At this time the parish priest relied heavily on the support of the ministers from the three main Protestant churches in the town. He worked closely with Church of Ireland rector Canon John McCarthy, the Rev. David Cupples of the Presbyterian Church, and Methodist minister the Rev. Tom Magowan. The monsignor says:

Somewhere along the line, about nine or ten o'clock on the night of the bomb, I became convinced that this had gone beyond us, it had become a worldwide event. It actually did become a world event so that now whatever part of the world you go to and you say you are from Enniskillen, they identify with the bomb.

Monsignor Cahill attended many funerals and was impressed by the forgiving nature of many of the families. As parish priest, he faced several days of intense questioning from reporters:

They would ask me how did Catholic people feel, and I said they felt revulsion and utter condemnation.

Then he was asked what would happen if a person told him in confession that he had done it.

I had heard the question asked before theoretically, but I had never dealt with it like this. I simply said confession is not a slot machine response to wrongdoing. Confession implies a total change of heart, a willingness to change one's ways. There is nothing automatic about forgiveness or reconciliation unless a person is prepared for a total change of heart.

The following day, Monsignor Cahill returned to the parochial house to find more than twenty journalists waiting for him. In a statement, he described the people who carried out the attack as 'barbarous and inhuman' and he urged Catholic families in the parish to give RUC detectives 'every possible assistance' in tracking down the bombers.

Much is made of the fact that the RUC is considered unacceptable in many Nationalist areas, and such an appeal was considered by some to be unprecedented. But Seán Cahill emphasises that it was not:

Normally we would have made that call. I remember every single incident here in the diocese of Clogher — Bishop Duffy issued a statement of condemnation, every single one.

The day after the bomb, the Standing Committee of Irish

Bishops of the Roman Catholic Church prepared a ten-point statement, which was sent to all parishes to be read at Masses. Among its points, the bishops said that recent events had evoked a new sense of revulsion and shame at the depth to which Ireland was being dragged:

> It is long since there has been such a sense of disgust throughout the Catholic community as Sunday's explosion in Enniskillen has aroused.
>
> There is in the Catholic community north and south a strong desire to find some way of collectively expressing our sympathy and solidarity with the Protestant community in this tragedy. Everything should be done to demonstrate Catholic revulsion at these crimes and to dissociate the Catholic community completely from those who carry out such deeds.
>
> There is no room for ambivalence. In face of the present campaigns of Republican violence the choice of all Catholics is clear. It is a choice between good and evil.
>
> It is sinful to join organisations committed to violence, or to remain in them. It is sinful to support such organisations or to call on others to support them.
>
> It has become clear that dotted across this country there are safe houses provided for members of these organisations. There are people who store weapons or who willingly help fugitives to escape. We say very solemnly to these people that they share in the awful crime of murder. People must choose. There is no longer any room for romantic illusion. There is no excuse for thinking that the present violence in Ireland can be morally justified.

It was as strong and unequivocal a statement as the Catholic hierarchy had produced.

The local Catholic bishop, the Most Rev. Dr Joseph Duffy, was in the south of France, but telephoned Monsignor Cahill to say that he would fly back immediately. Then Cardinal Tomás Ó Fiaich rang to say that he would be attending a special Mass arranged at St Michael's church for Thursday evening.

The cardinal arrived early and went for tea in the parochial house, but word had spread that he was there, and a steady stream of journalists arrived looking for interviews. The cardinal received them all and sat in the front room answering their questions.

Over a thousand people were waiting in the church for the Mass called especially to pray for the eleven Protestant victims of the IRA. There was an air of great expectancy before the start. Suddenly, everyone in the congregation burst into applause when Gordon Wilson walked in and took his seat, accompanied by local junior Methodist minister, the Rev. Derrick Haskins.

Bishop Duffy spoke of 'the serenity and spirit of forgiveness which shines so radiantly through the grief of those who are bereft'. Cardinal Ó Fiaich apologised to the Protestant community for attacks by people from his own community.

After the service, the cardinal met privately with Gordon Wilson. He also paid a visit to the Erne to visit some of the injured. He was well received, with the exception of one woman who verbally harangued him, claiming that the Catholic Church's people were responsible for the outrage.

However, relatives particularly were able to distinguish the difference between their Catholic neighbours and those who had carried out the attack. Margaret Veitch says:

> Our Roman Catholic friends were more than good. I knew they were genuinely aggrieved by what had happened. As well as ordinary Catholics coming to the house, we had priests and nuns; I found them a great comfort. Some Catholics asked my husband Crawford if I would speak to them, but of course I would. I knew they were hurt and annoyed too.

Aileen Quinton remembers a Roman Catholic neighbour telling her cousin at the chapel of rest that he would not be surprised if the family was very angry with him:

> But she just said, 'Oh, don't be silly, everybody knows good Catholics like you don't do things like this. Auntie Alberta would have been the first one to say that.' I don't feel any guilt over what the UVF do.

Ulster Unionist member of Fermanagh District Council, Raymond Ferguson, says that Enniskillen does not have the traditional bitterness between the two communities that many other towns in Northern Ireland have:

> I think the Catholic community certainly did not like their Protestant neighbours being attacked in this way. That came across to me more and more when I met people during the week. It was happening on a one-to-one basis throughout the town and they were clearly embarrassed by what was happening.

It would be foolish to claim that the feeling of unity between Catholics and Protestants in the town was universal. Free Presbyterian minister, the Rev Ivan Foster, issued a statement, which claimed, among other things, that 'effective measures against the terrorists are curtailed because it would bring a storm of protest from the Roman Catholic Church.' He claimed that the tragedy was being exploited by ecumenists to advance 'unity with Romanism'.

Support for the Injured

There was a steady flow of visitors to the Erne hospital. At four o'clock one morning, the Rev. Ian Paisley arrived and among those he prayed with was young Catherine Ross, who had received a head injury. Northern Ireland Office Government Minister Richard Needham visited patients including 6-year-old Lisa Cathcart. On Monday night, the hospital was informed that Prince Charles was taking a personal interest in the tragedy and would like to speak to one of the injured. Austin Stinson, who had suffered a broken pelvis when buried in the rubble, was asked if he would take a telephone call, and the conversation was set up for Tuesday morning.

All around, the support continued to be expressed — a silent vigil was organised, and hundreds of townspeople held hands in tribute. On the following Sunday, a service of remembrance was held in St Anne's Church of Ireland cathedral in Belfast. Among the 4,000 congregation was a group of Enniskillen children. When they entered the cathedral they were applauded by schoolchildren from all parts of Northern Ireland.

The Media

From an early stage, it was clear that Enniskillen was a major 'story'. The BBC and ITV encamped in Enniskillen for two weeks. The former took over a floor of the town's Railway Hotel and set up an editing suite, with journalists and production staff using it as a base to send back numerous reports. ITN took over Franco's restaurant in the town and did the same.

Throughout the week there were problems with the press, particularly photographers from the English tabloids. On one occasion a photographer was caught at the door of the hospital mortuary, while another day a photographer was spotted outside the surgical ward trying to take photos from outside of patients recovering from their injuries. However, those journalists who behaved irresponsibly were very much in the minority, and there was co-operation with those who requested permission.

Stephen Ross, the teenager who had hours of surgery to rebuild his face, was approached by photographer Trevor McBride in Derry. He agreed to be photographed and McBride's photo of the boy with a metal frame around his face was a memorable one.

James Mullan agreed to speak to a reporter from the *Chicago Tribune* about losing his parents. He told the reporter that the IRA might as well have put a bomb in a church because the ceremony was a religious occasion. The American paper used the line as its 'quote of the week'.

On the Sunday evening, Council Chief Executive Gerry Burns took part in an Ulster Television programme which attracted one of the station's highest-ever viewing figures. He had been at the cenotaph when the bomb went off and he was particularly conscious of the contribution he could make as a Catholic in a position of community responsibility:

> Inevitably there would be a massive reaction. It had been a cruel and wicked thing to do, the sort of thing that could very well have started a civil war. It was an attack on innocent people, guilty of nothing except trying to make their living. They were simply there, youngsters and adults, in an honourable act of remembering the dead who had given their lives in war, including fighting the terrible things of Nazi Germany.

Gerry Burns had been instrumental a few years before in persuading the BBC to set up a small radio studio in the town. Now it was being used to broadcast reports all over the world:

> Enniskillen was thrown into what was actually world coverage; there is no question about that because they were there from all sorts of countries. You couldn't go round a corner but you would run into a television crew or whatever. There were reporters everywhere wanting to do stories.

Canon John McCarthy recalls being in his office at ten o'clock on Monday evening when the BBC telephoned asking him to appear on the *Kilroy* programme, a studio discussion coming live from Belfast the following morning. He agreed to go when they guaranteed to have him back on time to speak at Sammy Gault's funeral in the afternoon. After midnight, a reporter from the *Belfast Telegraph* called at the deanery looking for an advance copy of his planned address at the funeral. He waited until two o'clock when the canon had finished writing it. Canon McCarthy finished other work at four in the morning. The BBC taxi called for him at half past six, and he was back in Enniskillen at lunchtime to conduct the funeral.

People generally felt happier in dealing with the Irish media. Reporters from Belfast and Dublin seemed to have a better understanding of the situation's sensitivities. A woman wrote from Ontario, Canada, to the Townhall saying how shocked she had been by one report there. Gerry Burns wrote back:

> It is regrettable that impressions should be given that we are standing in Northern Ireland in the midst of a religious war, with daggers drawn, unable to have any rapprochement by either side. This is far from the truth. Normal life continues, with people mixing, working and living together in a Christian spirit.

Mr Burns says that the reporter was 'ill-informed and over-zealous for a juicy story'.

However, it would be unfair to undermine some of the superb reporting of many others

Response from the Republic

The bombing itself and the coverage given to it resulted in a massive international response. Letters and messages poured in all week praising the honour and dignity of those directly affected and the courage shown by everyone in the week of funerals. The local MP, Ken Maginnis, says:

> I have no doubt that the reason Enniskillen grabbed the attention was quite simply throughout the whole of the United Kingdom and, indeed, further afield, people were doing exactly the same thing at the same time. The attack in Enniskillen was magnified thousands of times. Every town and village where that ceremony is held, people were standing silently when the bomb went off. Metaphorically, the sound of the bomb reverberated through that silence.

It seemed that people in the Republic of Ireland were particularly horrified. Raymond Ferguson says:

> In my opinion, one thing about the Enniskillen bomb which never got enough publicity was the way people in the Republic responded. They were horrified by it and wanted to distance themselves from it. They set up registers in an awful lot of towns and over 300,000 people took the trouble to go out and sign them. That is one in ten of

the population, a huge percentage; that probably works out at one in five or six of the adult population. It was an example of how the people in the Republic were horrified by the IRA campaign in general. It was very sincere.

On RTÉ's *Late Late Show*, Gay Byrne interviewed Fr Brian D'Arcy who recalled his schooldays in Enniskillen, and singer Chris de Burgh sang a song he had composed especially and dedicated to the people of Enniskillen, 'especially Marie' who had attended his concerts.

In Dublin, books of condolence were opened at the Lord Mayor's official residence, the Mansion House. The Lord Mayor at the time, Ms Carmencita Hederman, remembers people arriving 'in droves' to sign:

Big as the Mansion House is, we couldn't get people in and out quickly enough to sign, so we had to put more books and more tables outside on the forecourt. It was reasonably fine weather and I remember the queues, particularly at lunchtime.

We filled forty books. They were just ordinary Dublin people who felt very moved and upset about the whole thing and wanted to be associated in some way with the tributes. It was something so sad and it just gripped people. There was a surge of feeling. After the books closed there were people ringing up pleading with us that they were getting out of hospital early to come and sign the books.

By then, 45,000 Dubliners had signed.

A week after the bombing, a service of remembrance was held in St Patrick's Cathedral, Dublin, attended by Ms Hederman. The Taoiseach, Charles Haughey, was also among the thousands packed into the cathedral who heard the Church of Ireland Bishop of Clogher, the Right Rev. Brian Hannon, express the hope that the disaster would be a watershed:

Somehow, Remembrance Sunday 1987 has added not only a new dimension of horror, but also a new dimension of hope.

After the service, the Lord Mayor travelled north to Ennis-killen to deliver the books of condolence. She was accompanied by her husband, Billy, her 20-year-old daughter Wendy and the City Manager, Frank Feely.

Many bereaved relatives had accepted an invitation to a reception in the Erne hospital to meet the Lord Mayor, who was overcome with the emotion of the occasion and broke down and wept, unable to deliver her speech. She remembers:

> I just felt overcome by the whole thing; what brought it home to me was looking at my daughter who was the same age as Gordon Wilson's daughter who wasn't there with her father and mother.

In addition to the books of condolence, Dublin sent more practical support in the form of a cheque for £39,000 for the Enniskillen Appeal Fund.

Appeal Fund

The day after the atrocity, numerous telephone calls were made to Enniskillen Townhall from around the world. On the suggestion of the Dowager Lady Brookeborough, Gerry Burns decided to set up a fund as a means of channelling the offers of support. Mr Burns, who took the initiative in a personal capacity, says:

> Immediately I reckoned here was something that could be done. I was conscious that people wanted to identify with us, but I was also conscious that I didn't want to simply solicit contributions.

A number of local people were asked to sit on a board of trustees: the four local churchmen, Canon John McCarthy, the Rev. David Cupples, Monsignor Seán Cahill, and the Rev. Tom Magowan; one Unionist councillor, Raymond Ferguson, and one Nationalist, Jim Lunny (from the SDLP). Local Justice of the Peace Bertie McCaffrey acted as secretary, and Gerry Burns as treasurer.

In a television interview, Gerry Burns was asked about the role of the Sinn Féin chairman of Fermanagh District Council. He recalls:

> I simply responded by saying that the people of Enniskillen were honest, quiet and reserved people; they were currently in the midst of personal grief and that the first thing they wanted to do was to bury their dead with some honour and dignity and we could leave other matters for other times.

Donations to the fund started to pour in:

> We got cheques and bankdrafts from Pakistan, Australia, New Zealand, the United States, from Great Britain and a great many from the south of Ireland. I have to say in particular from the south. Many people arrived with memorial books of remembrance signed by thousands and thousands of people. Some schools in the south had taken some trouble to make lovely designs on the front. I thought all those things were lovely.

In addition to Dublin's £39,000, there were other large donations. The Duke of Westminster, whose family had a home in Co. Fermanagh, sent £10,000. Another £10,000 was received from the citizens of Bradford in England, where a number of people had been killed in a fire disaster at Bradford City football ground in 1985. Television personality David Frost donated the royalties from a book of short stories he had written.

Other donors included a disabled man from Belfast who undertook a sponsored tour of Northern Ireland, raising £3,000 for the fund; and two third formers — Damien Campbell at St Michael's College and Justin Keogh at Portora Royal School — who, in a cross-community effort, raised £203. The 'Loyalist prisoners of H block 4' sent £101.

Within days, the fund had received £125,000, and by the time it closed a few weeks later it had realised the sum of over £660,000.

Letters of Support

Just as welcome were the contributions from many ordinary people. Two people arrived from a fishing village in Co. Mayo in the west of Ireland with a book signed by all the villagers. They also brought a huge salmon which was donated to the hospital for the injured to enjoy. Food hampers were sent from London.

With the contributions came many touching messages. One was from Ian Gibb who had lost both parents in the Hungerford massacre, when gunman Michael Ryan had gone on a murderous rampage earlier that summer in the quiet south of England village. Mr Gibb wrote:

> Nothing can alleviate the suffering and pain of the sudden loss of a family member or a friend. But be assured you are all in our thoughts and prayers at this tragic time.

A woman from Huddersfield in England wrote simply:

> I was moved to write to let you know that there are many ordinary folk over here who feel powerless to do anything.

Other messages came from the Chevy Chase Presbyterian Church, Washington DC; the people of Saragossa, Spain; the Quaker community, Waterford; the Augustinian Church, Cork; and individuals from Belgium, Germany and the Netherlands.

Following the Rev. David Cupples' appearance on television, he received 500 letters in the week following the bomb, from friends and other Presbyterian congregations offering their prayers and support. A letter was received by the Enniskillen branch of the Royal British Legion from the wife of former British Conservative Party chairman, Norman Tebbitt. Mrs Tebbitt had been disabled when caught up in the IRA bombing of the Conservative Party Conference in Brighton in 1984. She wrote the letter herself, the shaky almost childlike handwriting a graphic illustration of her own injuries.

Gordon Wilson's interview resulted in 5,000 letters arriving at his home in the first week alone. Joan Wilson recalls answering the door one wet afternoon:

> I shall never forget this. These two elderly ladies had travelled on the bus from Dublin. They had walked up to the Rosses' house to leave sweets for the children and came on here to give their sympathy and a box of chocolates before going back on the bus to Dublin.

All the other families received messages of condolence and support too. A number of world figures offered their sympathy in a more public way, and added their condemnation. British Prime Minister Margaret Thatcher condemned the event as a 'blot on mankind'. Queen Elizabeth expressed her shock at the atrocity, adding: 'My heartfelt sympathy goes out to the bereaved and injured.' US President Ronald Reagan wrote to Mrs Thatcher passing on the sympathy of the American people. The Pope condemned it as a 'cruel act'. The Taoiseach, Charles Haughey, expressed his 'anger and revulsion'. The Queen Mother sent a telegram to the Queen's representative in Fermanagh, the Earl of Erne, asking him to pass on her sympathy to the county.

Condemnation came also from unexpected quarters. In Moscow, the official Soviet news agency, Tass, described the bombing as a 'barbaric act', and Libya, usually sympathetic to the IRA, sent criticism through its news agency, JAVA:

> This operation does not belong to legitimate revolutionary operations in the fight for liberation.

It seemed that the world wanted to identify with Enniskillen's suffering. Sammy Foster, a social worker seconded by the appeal trustees to work with the bereaved families and the injured, believes that in the initial days the mass media coverage and worldwide sympathy acted as a 'cushion'. He says:

> It helped in its own strange way to help people along in what was a great tide of emotion. In this area of death and bereavement, I believe we can all be clumsy. It is

indeed extremely sensitive. The reference in *The Little Prince* in 1945 is pertinent:

> 'I did not know what to say to him. I felt awkward and blundering. I did not know how I could reach him, where I could overtake him and go hand in hand with him once more. It is such a secret place, the land of tears.'

5: Learning to Live Again

The name of the town of Enniskillen is now known internationally. Many associate it with an awful day of death; but it is also remembered for the display of dignity by its townspeople when they came under the most intense media spotlight.

Just over a week later, a fire at King's Cross underground station in London caused that spotlight to be directed elsewhere. What some had referred to as the 'cushion' of media attention was removed and the people of Enniskillen were left to learn to live again. The difficulty was that different people had different needs.

Social worker David Bolton, contributing to an American book, *When a Community Weeps*, refers to this as 'hierarchies of suffering'. He explains:

> At the top of this there was a number of bereaved people. Then the injured, then the traumatised and then the great mass of ordinary folk. In a sense we asked the questions, 'Who does the disaster belong to? Does it belong to the families or does it belong to the community?' The answer, I think, is both but the two became interlocked.[1]

Two very public events played a major part in helping the community in general to pick up the pieces of their lives.

Royal Visit

Nine days after the bombing, there was a surprise visit to Enniskillen by the Prince and Princess of Wales. Prince

Charles had telephoned the Erne hospital two days after the bombing to speak to Austin Stinson, one of the injured. Days later, an intermediary contacted the authorities there on his behalf to say that he and Princess Diana would like to come as soon as possible. The hospital's district administrator, Norman Hilliard, was called to the RUC station late the night before the proposed visit, on Tuesday 17 November, and told: 'Tomorrow morning is on. Charles and Diana are coming.'

Mr Hilliard was in the hospital at six o'clock the following morning to make arrangements. A massive security operation needed to be in place by the time he and other administrative, nursing and medical staff met the Royals at half past eleven. Police marksmen with telescopic sights were perched on roofs around the town. The red Royal helicopter landed at St Angelo army base, and the Royal couple were driven the four miles to Enniskillen to visit the hospital, where they spent seventy minutes chatting to staff and patients injured in the bombing.

The Prince had spoken to Austin Stinson by telephone and now the couple came to visit him personally. The relaxed Princess sat on the edge of the bed and admired his Marks and Spencer pyjamas. Harry Donaldson remembers discussing with the Prince the virtues of drinking Guinness.

As the couple were moving down the corridor, one of the nurses nervously dropped her camera. A relaxed Prince Charles smiled and picked it up, commenting as he handed it back to her, 'That was a pity you missed your photograph.' Later, the same nurse was taking photos and he remarked, 'I see it's working again.'

Nathan Chambers remembers feeling excited about the visit of the Royal couple:

> I looked out of the hospital window that morning and there were marksmen all over the roof. We weren't supposed to know, but we soon found out that Prince Charles and Princess Diana were coming, so I sent Mum

and Dad out to get me a new autograph book. The first autograph in it was Prince Charles and the second was Princess Diana.

They came to the bed separately. Prince Charles was a bit more formal and harder to talk to. But Princess Diana was very down-to-earth, very friendly and very quiet. She was very concerned about my well-being and asked if there was anything she could do.

When Princess Diana was killed in a car crash in Paris on 31 August 1997, Nathan was one of hundreds of people to pay tribute to her in Enniskillen. He laid a bouquet of flowers in the town centre, and wrote a message on a card, thanking her for showing love and comfort 'at a time when I needed it most.'

The Prince and Princess also signed autographs for teenagers Clive Armstrong and Ian Carson, also injured in the blast. They signed their names in the front of a Bible for Daphne Stephenson who was also recovering from her injuries, and they chatted to Peter McBrien and Vernon Huey, the other two victims still in hospital. The Princess also cuddled baby Sara Ternan, born on the afternoon of the bombing.

Mr Hilliard recalls that prior to the visit, hospital staff morale had been very low. Some felt that the nursing and medical staff should have had more support in terms of counselling. However, according to Mr Hilliard, 'That visit really lifted morale and they never looked back afterwards.' Later, there would be further official recognition, with surgeon Andrew McKibben receiving an OBE in the British honours list, casualty department sister Jane Packham an MBE, and porter Pat Curry a BEM.

The Royal visit proved a massive fillip for the town as a whole. Word had spread and a large crowd had gathered outside as the couple left the hospital for the drive back to the army base, where a number of the bereaved, together with community leaders and those who had assisted in the rescue efforts, were waiting for a private meeting.

Ceremony Rearranged

After the visit, the town went on with its preparations for another event that would be significant in rebuilding morale. On Sunday, 22 November, Enniskillen held its Remembrance Sunday ceremony. Many thought that the parade and service were a memorial for the eleven victims. In fact, the ceremony was simply a restaging of the event that had been abandoned two weeks earlier in the chaos of the bomb attack.

On the afternoon of the bomb, the Church of Ireland rector, Canon John McCarthy, and Archbishop Robin Eames returned from the hospital to the rectory for a late lunch with Canon McCarthy's wife, Isobel. The Rector recalls:

> There were only the three of us, and I remember saying, just in the course of conversation, that I was going to have a service in a fortnight's time.

The Archbishop checked his diary and discovered another engagement, but was quickly persuaded that it could not be as important as this. Canon McCarthy explains:

> I just remember thinking, why should we allow them to say we are not going to remember the dead of two world wars? We are going to do it. I didn't realise it was going to turn out to be such a major occasion, but we were going to do it anyway.

The officers of the Enniskillen branch of the Royal British Legion were of like mind. At the time of the bomb, they had gone ahead with some parts of the ceremony: a few wreaths were laid at the far end of Belmore Street, and a party of four standard-bearers marched through the town centre to St Macartin's cathedral. They included the Legion's own flag, as well as the women's branch flag and the standards of the Royal Air Force Association and the Inniskilling Fusiliers Association. But most of their 100 ex-servicemen did not parade.

Willie Scarlett, chairman of the British Legion branch,

called an emergency meeting that evening in the organisation's hall in Enniskillen. The dozen members of the
committee were in sombre mood as they gathered in a
side room. Willie Scarlett recalls:

> Everybody was in a state of shock. We had to decide what
> we were going to do. We all felt that our day was can-
> celled due to the bomb, so we should go ahead and have
> it at a later date. We felt the appropriate time would be a
> fortnight later. The re-run was to be the same as the or-
> dinary Remembrance Day.

However, the ninety British Legion branches in Northern
Ireland indicated that on this occasion, as they had al-
ready held their own ceremonies, they would come to
Enniskillen to display their support. Northern Ireland
Legion organiser, Douglas Wilkie, took charge of the
arrangements.

With many other visitors also intending to come, it
became clear that this would not be an ordinary
Remembrance Sunday. Instead of the usual 500 people,
there were over 5,000 packed into the narrow Belmore
Street, with millions more watching on television. ITV and
BBC had decided to show the ceremony live throughout
the United Kingdom, and RTÉ showed it live in the
Republic.

The Prime Minister Arrives

There had been speculation throughout the week that a
VIP would attend. Some expected a member of the Royal
family, but the identity remained a secret until the last
minute. The level of security gave no clue, having been
stepped up to unprecedented levels anyway. On the Saturday night, police and troops with sniffer dogs
conducted a thorough search of houses and shops along
the planned parade route. Pubs and places of entertain-
ment were cleared early, and traffic was banned from the
town centre from half past eight on Sunday morning.

Even the Legion officers were not informed of the

identity of the VIP. Willie Scarlett recalls:

> We knew somebody of importance was coming, but we
> didn't know whether it was Royalty or the Prime Minister.
> We were gathering in the car park before moving off for
> the parade when word came through that it was the
> Prime Minister. They kept it very closely, we didn't know
> until the last minute.

The identity of the visitor had been revealed to Canon
McCarthy when an official had called at midnight to tell
him to make arrangements for seating at the following
morning's service.

According to Sir Bernard Ingham, Mrs Thatcher's
press secretary who accompanied her on the visit to
Enniskillen, there was never any doubt about her coming. Although she had to be in France on Sunday evening
for a meeting with President Mitterand, she was determined to go to Enniskillen. Sir Bernard explains:

> She went all the time wherever the IRA struck. She went
> in order to demonstrate her solidarity with the people,
> with the bereaved and with the injured. She went to
> demonstrate that there was simply no way in which she
> was going to give in on this.

He goes on to say that Mrs Thatcher took Remembrance
Sunday very seriously:

> She regarded that as a very solemn Prime Ministerial
> duty — never to forget the sacrifices. For this to happen
> on that occasion in Enniskillen when, let's face it, Catho-
> lic and Protestant, Ulster men and Republic of Ireland
> soldiers were being honoured, she thought that was a
> pretty grim example of terrorism at work.

Mrs Thatcher herself recalls the horror she felt when told
of the bombing. On being informed that I was writing this
book, she wrote to me early in 1997. Her letter states:

> I heard the first news of the attack at the reception which
> follows the Remembrance Day service at the Cenotaph [in
> London] and could not believe that anyone would be

capable of committing such an act of unremitting evil. Of all the atrocities inflicted on the people of Ulster, the act of merciless savagery against the people of Enniskillen stands out in its infamy.

A fortnight later, the British Prime Minister travelled to stand beside the disintegrated building where the IRA had carried out the attack. She landed by helicopter at St Angelo, and a briefing was held with senior army and RUC officers. Mrs Thatcher and her husband, Denis, were then driven to the town in a black limousine, accompanied by an elaborate motorcade, including officials and Special Branch officers. The streets were devoid of any other vehicles.

As the Prime Minister alighted at the War Memorial, Ballyreagh Silver Band struck up 'God Save the Queen' — a breach of protocol as it should only be done for members of the Royal family. However, nobody seemed to mind, and Mrs Thatcher, looking solemn and dressed in black with a red poppy on her lapel, was led to her place beside Fermanagh Councillor Raymond Ferguson. She was accompanied by Northern Ireland Secretary of State, Tom King, wearing his war medals.

Ballyreagh Silver Band bugler David Fyffe recalls that it was a foul morning, cold and wet, but Mrs Thatcher had declined the offer of an umbrella. He has particular reason to keep an eye on the weather, as in the ceremony he has to sound the last post. He says:

> You just go for it and either hit the note or not. It doesn't help when it is cold and wet like it was that morning. I watched Mrs Thatcher and she didn't flinch. She must be made of steel.

Fluttering in the strong breeze that morning were 170 flags, mostly Royal British Legion standards from branches that had marched along Belmore Street. The Legion standard is a distinctive royal blue and yellow flag, which made it an even more striking scene. As the band played, the rain relented and a rainbow appeared in the sky.

Bomb Alert

With a few minutes left before eleven o'clock, a number of relatives of people killed a fortnight before stood gathered in one corner. Many of the hundreds packed on all sides around the War Memorial had also been there two weeks before. They felt a mixture of emotions, including fear. Sammy Foster, who had pulled some of the dead out, was standing behind Mrs Thatcher with the chief executive of the Council and a group of other councillors. He remembers:

> I happened to notice a bit of a fuss in the entry between Follis's and McNulty's shops a few yards over to the right. This police inspector came over and I heard him say that a phone call had been received claiming there was a bomb in McNulty's. Honestly, I didn't know whether to run or what. That was scary. We didn't want to make a scene, but it was frightening. After what happened the last time, I was waiting to see the whole building go up. But they kept it cool, there was no big fuss.

In fact, several hoax calls were received. But the security forces had searched the area so thoroughly and put such a ring of security round the town that it was decided not to disrupt the ceremony. Discreet checks were carried out, and the solemn ceremony went ahead.

The Ceremony

The Queen's representative in the county, the Earl of Erne, was led to his place, and the two minutes' silence were observed. The Remembrance Sunday homily pays homage to those who died in war, saying: 'When you go back, tell them, for your tomorrow we gave our today.' And later, there is the exhortation:

> They shall grow not old, as we that are left grow old. Age shall not weary them, nor the years condemn. At the going down of the sun and in the morning, we will remember them.

The format on this occasion was as normal, with no official reference to the bomb victims. The wreath-laying was led by Lord Erne, followed by the Prime Minister, who then moved off and was driven to St Macartin's Rectory. The ceremony in Belmore Street continued, with wreaths being laid by local organisations, including many schools and youth organisations. Then the parade of bands and ex-servicemen and women moved through the town towards the courthouse where Lord Erne traditionally takes the salute.

Knowing that this would take almost half an hour, officials had asked Canon McCarthy to entertain Mrs Thatcher for a short time before the service. He recalls:

> She was driven up to the back door of the rectory and I remember because it was such a bad day she was soaked. My wife Isobel had to get an electric heater and Mrs Thatcher took her shoes off and was standing in the front room drying her feet.

The Prime Minister declined the offer of tea and the small group of eight people, including some officials, stood around chatting — Canon McCarthy in his white robe ready to conduct the service, and Mrs Thatcher in her stocking feet. The rector says:

> In that setting she struck me as being quite humble really. I told her we appreciated the fact that she came, especially as she was so busy. I think I spoke for the people of Enniskillen because I think her visit was deeply appreciated. She said she was glad to be there. She was determined to come, even though she had to meet the President of France that afternoon.

Canon McCarthy then escorted Mrs Thatcher and her husband Denis into the Church of Ireland cathedral, in which all 700 seats had been allocated. Rector's churchwarden Gordon Jackson was in charge of the arrangements, and he hurried up the aisle to inform Canon McCarthy that Lord Gerry Fitt had arrived unexpectedly. A seat was found for him in a side pew beside Fianna Fáil

TD for Louth, Brendan McGahan.

However, the majority of those in the cathedral were local people, relatives of those killed and members of the British Legion. Archbishop Eames returned to preach and spoke on the theme of Matt 5: 'Blessed are the peacemakers for they shall be called the children of God.'

After the service, Mrs Thatcher briefly met some of the bereaved relatives, and some British Legion officers, including the chairman, Willie Scarlett. In her letter to me, recalling the day, Mrs Thatcher wrote:

> I shall always remember the emotional service in St Macartin's Cathedral. The courage and determination of local people, many of whom had been injured or lost loved ones, gave eloquent answer to the terrorists. The bomb and the bullet were no match for their quiet dignity.

Significance of Mrs Thatcher's Presence

Far from being simply a good photo opportunity, as one journalist had suggested, Mrs Thatcher's presence in Enniskillen that day speaks volumes about the British Establishment's attitude to Northern Ireland, according to Sir Bernard Ingham:

> They say the English don't understand the Irish. But I think for the last thirty years, the Irish have never understood the English. We will not be bombed out, we have a peculiar sense of duty which prohibits us from doing so. I think that these events merely strengthen the resolve. The IRA picked a wrong 'un in her and they ought to have known it.

Sir Bernard Ingham is blunt about his own personal view on Northern Ireland:

> If only you could sink the bloody place in the middle of the Atlantic it would be a very great bonus for the British people. We have had enough, but what stops us washing our hands of it and running away is a duty, a responsibility. Firstly, there is the possibility of a blood bath and

secondly there is a democratic expression on the part of the majority including many Catholics who wish to remain part of the United Kingdom. If you are a democrat, you have to observe a democratic vote. There is no point in saying you would love to dump it at the bottom of the ocean if you are flying in the face of a democratically expressed opinion.

He stresses, however, that he never heard the Prime Minister say anything to suggest that she would wish to be rid of Northern Ireland:

I don't think she ever kidded herself that she was going to be terribly successful in Northern Ireland. But I think that what the Anglo–Irish Agreement in 1985 demonstrated was that, notwithstanding her uncompromising attitude towards terrorism, she was prepared to keep trying. But incidents like Enniskillen were not merely futile, they were counter-productive, worse than futile.

As Mrs Thatcher's press secretary for eleven years, Sir Bernard saw her toughness of character:

I think she was especially tough with anybody who sought to overthrow democracy. She was especially tough with Arthur Scargill. But I think the difference with Scargill was that people were not being murdered. As far as the IRA was concerned, if they had any doubts about her commitment to democracy and willingness to stand up to dictators, then they learned early in the years of the hunger strike.

He believes that her attitude to Enniskillen was:

a mix of compassion and resolve — compassion with the people who suffer but an uncompromising determination on no account to allow that compassion to interfere with the fight that had to go on.

It increased her contempt for the kind of person who would do that. They had slaughtered innocents all along the line and I suppose she was pleased that the IRA came out of it badly. The IRA will defeat themselves in the end.

Catharsis

The rearranged Remembrance Sunday ceremony has been described in Enniskillen as a catharsis, the start of a process which enabled the community to purge itself of grief and begin to live again. ITV interspersed Sir Alastair Burnett's commentary on the ceremony with interviews with local people. One man said: 'I feel things are going to change after this.' Another expressed the hope that children would grow up in peace, and said: 'I hope that they will say that this was the time the violence stopped.'

The visit of the Prince and Princess of Wales and the re-arranged ceremony of remembrance had helped in some way to lift the community, so that people could begin to hope again.

Social worker David Bolton and teachers Toni Johnson and Kate Doherty were also helping people to cope. Mrs Johnson was a teacher in Enniskillen High School and had seen that many of her pupils were deeply affected, some through personal injury, some through being witnesses to the awful events, and many simply through knowing people who had been injured or killed.

Mrs Johnson remembered an experience her own daughter, Rachael, had had eight years previously. In August 1979, when Rachael was 16, she had been on holiday in Mullaghmore in Co. Sligo. Lord Mountbatten, a member of the Royal Family, was on holiday there too, and was on his boat in Sligo Bay when an IRA bomb exploded, killing four people including Lord Mountbatten, his 14-year-old grandson Nicholas, the Dowager Lady Brabourne and 15-year-old Enniskillen boy, Paul Maxwell.

Rachael was a close friend of the Maxwell family and was standing with Paul's sister, Donna, when they witnessed the boat being blown to pieces. Mrs Johnson recalls that Rachael talked her nightmare through time and again, saying:

> It was just like an exploding matchbox with tiny pieces of wood drifting down from the sky. I could feel the wind on my face.

Above: Men, women and children flee the scene of the bombing.

Below: Minutes after the explosion, the body of one of the victims has already been removed from the rubble and laid to one side.

Above: Scene of Destruction: Rescue workers at the collapsed gable wall of the Reading Rooms.

Below: An injured man is comforted by rescuers.

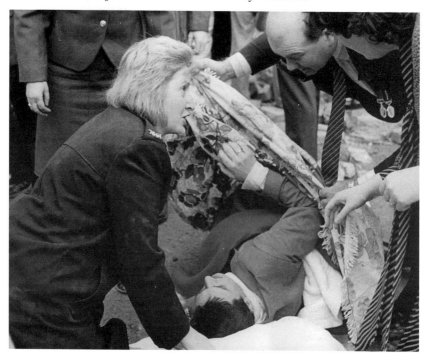

There were three married couples among the dead:

Top: Jessie and Kit Johnston at Hillsborough Castle when Kit received his British Empire Medal;

Middle: Wesley and Bertha Armstrong;

Bottom: William and Nessie Mullan.

Also among the dead:

Top: (L) Johnny Megaw,
aged 67; (R) Alberta Quinton,
aged 72.

Middle: (L) Samuel Gault,
aged 49;
(R) Edward Armstrong, aged 52.

Bottom: Marie Wilson, aged 20.

The town buries its dead: *Above*: The funeral of Sammy Gault leaves St Macartin's Cathedral, Enniskillen. His widow, Gladys, is comforted by relatives.

Below: The funeral cortège of Marie Wilson passes the scene of the explosion on its way to the cemetery.

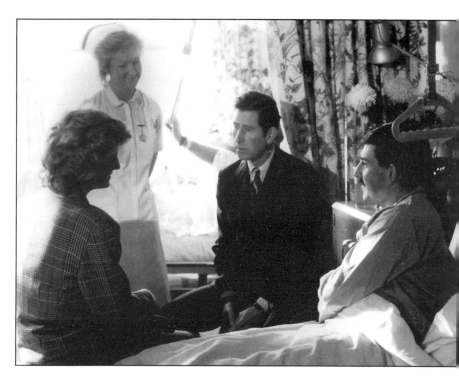

Above: Prince Charles and Princess Diana visit injured victim Austin Stinson at the Erne Hospital, Enniskillen.

Left: Enniskillen's War Memorial, with the doves added in 1991 as a tribute to those killed in the atrocity.

Injury victim Jim Dixon:

Right: As he was before the bombing.

Below: Weeks afterwards with serious facial injuries.

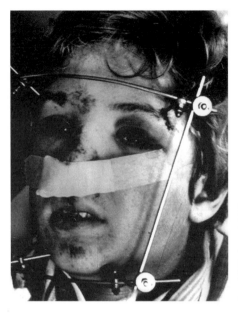

Injury victim Stephen Ross:

Left: His face wired after more than five hours of surgery.

Below: As he is today.

She remembers discussing this after the Remembrance Sunday bombing:

> We were talking about this in school and one of the teachers said that she felt we ought to talk the children through this, but it was difficult because they were all different ages. We also felt it would have been difficult for them to talk to their parents because their parents were thinking, 'Oh it could have been you, don't talk about it.' So we were afraid that these children would lock things into their head.

After a few days, all the children who had been at the War Memorial were brought into a classroom and given paper and pens. They were told to write down exactly what had happened and what they had seen. Toni Johnson watched them:

> There was total silence. They wrote and wrote without any punctuation. They just wrote as if it was getting it out of themselves. They were the most moving accounts, but it was strange because they were like pictures — they saw everything in detail. One little boy gave a sigh and pushed the paper away when he finished as if he had unloaded.

One girl wrote:

> On Sunday morning at 10 20 mum Shirley Julie Andrew and I left the house with Julies father in the car we got as far as the library we had to walk from there in front of us Sammy Gault and Stephen Gault walked to the war memorial and we stood at railings at the time the time was 10 35 Sammy said to mum do you think it will keep dry for the service and mum said I hope it does and mum saw Ian Johnston and said come on over here until I ask Ian about his father who was in hospital with chest pains Ian went on after talking to mum and mum said we might as well stay here and then Linda Black and a woman called Cissy came up to talk to us and mum said to Linda look at your feet and look at mine we have the same shoes on and I saw a flash of lightening and felt something like a wind and then I heard a bang and I think black dust came all around us and there were bricks and glass flying

through the air towards us and then I saw a brick coming towards me and it hit me on the side of the neck mum caught on to me and then let go I can remember running up the road and holding the right side of my neck and I saw Shirley and Andrew and I ran to them I also saw Cissy and I helped her out of the dust a man came along and brought me to the Horseshoe Bar and Mrs Coalter brought Shirley and Andrew and I to the hospital and mum came up a few minutes later it happened on the 8th of November 1987.

One of the teachers asked a girl whether she felt angry about what had happened and she replied, 'No, you just feel sad.'

As time went on, it became clear that other pupils had more problems. One girl, absent for two weeks with hearing problems caused by the blast, was very traumatised. She would cry and grind her teeth, even gnawing through a gum shield intended to protect them. Another younger girl had problems sleeping, cried a lot and wet her bed.

The children were also thinking of their headmaster, Ronnie Hill, who was still in a coma. Vice-principal Vic Outram kept them up to date with his condition and the pupils made flowers to send. Each pupil made one flower from paper to be mounted on a huge card.

People were brought in from organisations such as CRUSE bereavement counsellors to talk the children through their experiences. Schools in Northern Ireland have a raised awareness of bereavement, and in recent years it has become a part of the curriculum for counsellors to come in to talk to children about death and dying. With pupils living in an area where a terrorist campaign has gone on for almost thirty years, inevitably, there are times when it affects them directly.

In addition to specific action with those most directly affected after the Enniskillen bombing, efforts were made to enable the school in general to cope. The school formal dance was cancelled that year, but otherwise efforts were made to get back to normal.

However, events in other areas often saw psychological problems return. For example, children came into school very upset by the images they saw on television of the brutal killings of two British soldiers caught up in a funeral in Belfast. Kate Doherty, now principal at Enniskillen Collegiate Girls School, remembers one pupil reacting very badly to seeing accounts of an attack on a busload of soldiers killed on their way back to Co. Tyrone from leave.

In a paper written for *Pastoral Care*, Kate Doherty says that it was assumed that people who escaped injury and whose family had not been injured would recover quickly after the initial shock. This proved not to be the case:

> First of all, it was amazing how many children had connections with the families most affected. Perhaps we should not have been surprised, given our small community. It was like a stone thrown into a pond with the ripples going out in ever-widening circles. Unless careful and sensitive investigating took place, it was possible to overlook children who carried the effect of the disaster with them somewhere in their lives.
>
> From my own experience in school, one of the girls most deeply affected by the tragedy was a senior pupil who had been at the cenotaph when the bomb exploded. When the dust cleared, her first instinct was to get away to a place of safety as quickly as possible. As she ran, she saw a younger fellow-pupil in great distress because she had lost her younger brother and was searching frantically for him. The senior girl ran on, and what was to haunt her in the weeks and months ahead was a feeling of intense guilt that she had not stopped to help. The fact that the young boy was later found safe did nothing to assuage those guilt feelings, which came to a head some three to four months after the bombing.[2]

For some who seemed to have suspended their reaction, the brutality of later events brought home to them the brutality of Enniskillen. Miss Doherty says:

> I found it was in the Spring, months afterwards, that some people came to light who were really still having a

great deal of distress and who needed a lot of reassurance and a lot of support. I think some of them were finding it hard to concentrate, some were finding it hard to sleep at night, some just quite tearful.

In addition to working with the children, there was support needed for the rest of the community. Toni Johnson and Kate Doherty were asked to attend meetings organised for the families and the injured. These did not take place until months afterwards but Miss Doherty says:

> I remember just feeling that I was dealing with raw people who were hurting so badly. It was all so sensitive.

David Bolton was assistant principal social worker in the area at the time. He was helping out at the hospital on the day of the bomb and personally knew many of those injured and killed. He says, 'I had a profound sense of the need to do something.' His instinct in the early days was that there should be a careful balance between being available for people who wanted help and yet not being too intrusive:

> There was no help offered during the first week. Most of the pastoral support came from the clergy. Knowing what I know now about these things, I think that was quite in order because it is most inappropriate to offer counselling at that sort of point. The full reality of what happened begins to take a grip about three or four months later. CRUSE, the bereavement organisation said this to us and almost to the day after three months we began to notice all was not well with some people.

In an article, 'After the Disaster', Aileen Quinton, whose mother Alberta was one of those killed, writes that the first three weeks were the easiest time of the next three years.[3]

Stress and Trauma

David Bolton has worked tirelessly for the community over the past ten years, to the extent that the stress complicated a stomach illness he had, and he needed surgery.

He says that in the days following the disaster, social services in Enniskillen acted in support of the normal mechanisms, such as the churches, schools, families, the clergy and youth organisations. A leaflet prepared at the time of the Bradford City football ground fire disaster was rewritten. It was called *Coping with a Major Personal Crisis*, and 12,000 copies were printed and distributed around Fermanagh.

He feels that people's faith was also very important in helping them to cope:

> I think people going through the experience of grief and loss felt supported from a source that was beyond them and they attributed that to God and gave thanks to God for that. They don't know how they got through it but they did. So in that sense I think people were changed. These events are life changing; there is no doubt about that.

At the time of the Enniskillen bombing, a new term had entered the lexicon of social workers and the medical profession — 'post traumatic stress'. David Bolton says:

> The first time I ever heard it being talked about was fol-lowing Hungerford the previous August. British research into stress and trauma was only at the margins. It is ten years back and our knowledge in the meantime has just mushroomed, it has grown enormously.

The lessons learned in dealing with Enniskillen have been used elsewhere:

> People have rung us up when disasters happened else-where and sought our views. We have offered help in other situations, some of which has been accepted, some which hasn't.

He stresses the importance of thinking in the long term:

> When there is a death, there is a lot of support. You have the wake, all the visits and the cards and the invitations

out to dinner. After a while that begins to tail off and then the reality begins to grow.

One of the difficulties facing people giving support was that there was a clear distinction between the grief felt by the families and injured and that felt by the wider community:

> Sometimes the way in which a community responds is different from what families and individuals need. I found in the very early days that people who were at a distance from Enniskillen were responding politically. The people who spoke loudest about locking people up and letting the security forces free and closing the Border were not the people of Enniskillen. They were the politicians and fireside commentators from outside.

The wider community of Enniskillen did respond positively. A peace vigil was held in the town, and a large crowd of people from both communities gathered to pay tribute on a dark November evening.

The Christmas lights at the east end of Enniskillen remained switched off in 1987 and the occasion was rather more subdued than usual. However, events such as the Royal visit and the rearranged Remembrance Sunday ceremony had focused attention and helped the wider community of Enniskillen to get back to business as usual. For the bereaved and injured though, life could never be the same.

---

1   Bolton, D. (1988): 'The Threat to Belonging in Enniskillen' in E.S. Zinner and M.B. Williams (Eds), *When a Community Weeps. Case Studies in Group Survivorship*, Washington DC: Taylor and Frances (forthcoming).

2   Doherty K. (1991): Article in *Pastoral Care* (The quarterly magazine of the National Association of Pastoral Care in Education), September: 29–33.

3   Quinton, A. (1996): 'After the Disaster' in *Welfare World* (The Journal of the Association of Welfare Workers in England), September: 5–9.

6: The Target

There has been considerable controversy regarding the intention of the IRA on 8 November 1987 at Enniskillen. According to the IRA, the attack was a 'mistake'. The organisation claims that deliberately killing what it terms as civilians has never been part of its war. Whoever was being targeted, what is certain is that the IRA intended to kill, and the operation was a well-planned one, like the hundreds carried out in Fermanagh in the past twenty-seven years.

The IRA in South Fermanagh

The IRA is strong along the Fermanagh Border and into Monaghan, Cavan, Leitrim and south Donegal. The 'South Fermanagh' brigade takes in a large geographical area, from Garrison in the south-west of the county across to Lisnaskea and southwards to Roslea. As IRA members do not recognise the Border, the brigade also takes in a swathe of north Monaghan and Leitrim. A number of IRA men on the run from the northern security forces are believed to live in Co. Monaghan, including some from east Tyrone. A number of hiding places for arms dumps and training camps have been uncovered in isolated Border areas of the Republic.

One of the IRA's leading players in the 1970s and 1980s, Seamus McElwaine, hailed from Scotstown in Co. Monaghan. He led an active service unit on a number of missions before being captured, with others, by the SAS near Roslea in 1980. He was convicted of the separate murders of a UDR man and an RUC Reservist. McElwaine escaped from the Maze prison in 1983 and remained on the run until 1986, when he again clashed with the SAS. On this occasion, he was shot dead by the undercover British troops.

While ambushes by IRA units to shoot locally based UDR and RUC personnel were common, another tactic used was to plant booby-trap bombs under their vehicles or to plant land mines beside roads, which would blow up when patrols passed over them.

With home-based volunteers and a number of northerners on the run, South Fermanagh has a considerable amount of experience and expertise in various types of guerrilla warfare. Prior to 1987, bombs were often made up with commercial explosive, but it was becoming more difficult to obtain. Sympathisers used to secrete it from quarries until regulations were tightened. Commercial explosive is much more powerful than the home-made variety, so less weight of commercial material was needed. As regulations became tighter, the IRA began to import large supplies of Semtex, an extremely powerful explosive, which was hard to detect.

However, for Enniskillen in 1987, the material used was 'home-made' explosives: a mixture of fertiliser and petrol. The bomb maker was clearly an expert because the forty-pound bomb was effective and left little residue.

The Enniskillen Bomb

The following account of the IRA operation has been compiled with information obtained from a number of sources who, for obvious reasons, cannot be named. I believe it to be accurate, but as long as those who planned and carried out the operation remain silent, this account cannot be definitively verified.

The Enniskillen bomb was manufactured in the Ballinamore area of Co. Leitrim. While the South Fermanagh

Brigade made it up, the help of other units was required in bringing it across the Border and placing it in the Reading Rooms building beside the War Memorial in Enniskillen in the heart of Fermanagh.

Firstly, intelligence had to be gathered about the intended target, including reports on what went on at Remembrance Day, and who attended the ceremony. Enniskillen town, although now famous in IRA history, has little record since the 1970s of having its own ASU (active service unit). But two Enniskillen men provided the information needed. The ceremony is a public one and extensively covered in the local papers, so information was gleaned relatively easily. The IRA would also have been briefed on the layout of the Reading Rooms building and how to gain access to it. A member of the IRA team due to plant the bomb visited Enniskillen and was shown around the area by one of the locals. He was given a rundown on how to get in and out of the Reading Rooms quickly.

With the bomb made up and the information all gathered, the journey to put the plan into action began in Co. Leitrim late on Friday night. This is where members of the West Fermanagh Brigade, based in the Ballyshannon–Bundoran area, came in to assist. The journey from Ballinamore to Enniskillen would normally take about an hour, but driving straight there with a bomb on board would involve considerable risk. The RUC and British Army, including the local UDR, often set up road checks without warning, and known Republicans are certain to have their vehicle searched.

To avoid this, the journey was undertaken in relays, with 'scouts' moving on ahead to ensure that the route was clear before the bomb team proceeded. Taking into account the bomb makers, the team to plant it, the Enniskillen involvement and the scouts along the route, up to thirty people were involved in some way in carrying out the entire operation.

By early on Saturday, the bomb was already on the outskirts of Enniskillen. It is not clear precisely when it was brought into town, but by late Saturday night or early Sunday morning it was in place inside the Reading

Rooms. This was achieved quickly and efficiently. The two Enniskillen men who had provided the vital information were used again, this time to guide the four-man bomb team in. This ended the local involvement. The gang would need just fifteen minutes to get to Belmore Street and just a couple of minutes to set the bag in a cupboard on a landing behind the gable wall. Two men were involved, one keeping watch and the other setting the bag in place. A few seconds were needed to make the minor adjustments which left the device primed and ready.

The building where the bomb was planted was old and dilapidated. It had limited use but one of its functions was to host a Saturday night bingo session. About fifty people, including a number of housewives, played there on Saturday night, 7 November 1987. They began shortly after nine o'clock and finished at half past ten. The bingo hall is on the middle floor of the three-storey building and the door to it is close to where the bomb was placed. A landing outside the room ran across to stairs to the top floor which was never used. Under the stairs is a small box room where the bag containing the bomb was placed.

After the bingo session ended, the building's caretaker, Jim Dunlop, left his children home to another part of town and went back to play cards with three other men in the basement, a short flight of stairs down from the bingo hall. Mr Dunlop joined Eamon Goodwin, Damien McGurn and Seamus McCarney in a game. Seamus's teenage son, also Seamus, stayed on too, having helped his father distribute bingo cards earlier. After a couple of hands, Seamus senior headed home.

Around midnight, Damien McGurn and Eamon Goodwin thought they heard noises coming from the bingo hall upstairs. The men went quiet for a moment, but the noise stopped. Creaking and odd sounds were commonplace in the old building on a winter's night. Ten minutes later, they heard the sound again. It was like footsteps. Eamon Goodwin went to the door and looked up the stairs but saw nothing and went back to playing cards.

The men finished their game at twenty to one in the morning and walked out together. As the caretaker took out his keys to the outside door, Eamon Goodwin paused briefly and shouted into the darkness in the direction of the bingo hall. 'If anybody's there, we're locking up.' There was silence. The card players dispersed and Jim Dunlop locked the outside door, which had been open, as was the usual practice on a busy Saturday evening when it was left open until everyone left.

The mystery of the footsteps at midnight has never been solved. It is in keeping with the circumstances of the IRA operation that this was the bomber at work.

Timer

The type of device was unusual in that a timer was used although the aim was to kill. Bombs can be detonated by a command wire leading to the device, by radio remote-control signal, or by placing a timer, which causes a connection to be made when it clicks on time. Usually when the aim is to kill, remote control (either a command wire or radio signal) is used. The bombers sit at a vantage point watching their bomb's location. The exact second their intended target passes it, they press the signal to detonate. For example, in January 1987 in Enniskillen, a bomb was put in a litter bin in High Street to attack a passing police patrol at night. The bombers parked off a side street in an area called Paget Square, watching policemen on the beat through the closed shopping area. When a policeman's reflection was clearly seen in a large plate-glass window opposite the bin, the bomb was detonated. Reserve Constable Ivan Crawford was killed.

After eleven civilians had been killed at Enniskillen, the first IRA statement to be issued claimed that a similar remote control device had been used, but that the bomb had been triggered early by British Army radio equipment scanning the area. Forensic finds quickly disproved this. British Army bomb experts revealed that small fragments of wire found in tonnes of rubble had been pieced together to prove that an electronic timer was used. The bomb had been set to go off at 10.43.

Timers are usually used to bomb specific property targets. Volunteers plant the bomb, set the timer and leave in good time. Once they leave, they have no more control over the bomb. If they are going to give a warning, this happens later. Warnings are usually not given in cases where the target will blow up without endangering people.

Using a timer in an attempt to kill people can be dangerously inaccurate for two reasons. Even with an electronic timer such as was used at Enniskillen, where the technology is similar to that used to programme video recorders, there is no absolute guarantee that it will go off at the precise second it is primed to go off. Neither is there any guarantee that the human target will pass by at the time expected by the bombers.

A timer had been used by the IRA in its attack on the British Conservative Party conference at the Grand Hotel, Brighton, in 1984. Among the delegates staying overnight were Prime Minister Margaret Thatcher and leading members of her Cabinet. The bomb exploded as planned in the middle of the night, killing five people, although Margaret Thatcher was not among them.

At Enniskillen in 1987, a number of people vital to the parade were late for various reasons. However, even if they had moved off on time, it is unlikely that the UDR soldiers would have reached the corner by 10.43.

So, what exactly was the IRA mistake? There are four main alternatives:

1. The target was the UDR and the intention was not to kill civilians, but the setting or placing of the timer went badly wrong;

2. The target was the UDR and the intention was not to kill civilians, but the intelligence gathered about the parade's timetable and layout was inaccurate;

3. The target was the UDR, but the IRA was prepared to risk some civilians to get at them — in which case the

mistake related, as in the first alternative, to the setting or placing of the device, or as in the second, to the information on the timetable and layout of the ceremony;

4. The aim was to kill whoever happened to be attending the occasion, including civilians — in which case the mistake lay not in the execution of the operation, but in the miscalculation of the outrage it would cause (this will be dealt with more fully in Chapter 10).

Republican Comment

The IRA has consistently refused to talk about Enniskillen, apart from brief statements at the beginning in which members said that it was a mistake and that they do not target civilians. Sinn Féin president Gerry Adams accepts the IRA explanation that its target was UDR men.

The following are some of the responses I got from other Republican sources who refused to be named:

> You have to understand how difficult it is for Republicans to talk about Enniskillen.

> The feeling is that it was a bad mistake, but it is over and done with. There is no point in talking about it now.

> Mistakes were made. In an organisation such as this, there is the potential for fuck-ups. That may be cold comfort to the families, but the fact is the result was obviously not intended.

In a conversation I had with one Republican, I tried to equate the victims of the Enniskillen bomb with the victims of Bloody Sunday in Derry, whose relatives are campaigning for a British apology for the death of fourteen civilians. His reply was:

> There is no comparison. Bloody Sunday was a deliberate act of murder carried out by the British under instruction from their government. Enniskillen was a mistake by amateur soldiers.

This man insisted that he was not putting a spin on

events, and that this was his sincerely held belief. Other Republicans I spoke to said that volunteers have privately expressed the reservation that they did not think that their war would result in such civilian casualties.

The fact that the IRA has remained tight-lipped about Enniskillen is an indication of the embarrassment caused to the Republican movement by the consequences. This will be discussed in detail in Chapter 10.

Reading Rooms Not Searched

While the spotlight was clearly on the IRA following the Enniskillen bomb, a vital question was being asked — why had the building in which the bomb was planted not been searched in advance? Free Presbyterian Church minister, the Rev. Ivan Foster, claimed that soldiers and policemen on the ground had been instructed not to search the Reading Rooms before the parade because of objections from the Roman Catholic Church.

Enniskillen parish priest, Monsignor Seán Cahill, gives his response to the claim:

> It was a total lie, totally untrue to say that we refused to have the hall searched. If I remember correctly, my house has been searched and the church itself has been searched in the past. When I heard the claim, I felt angry. But I wasn't enormously moved by it because I simply knew it wasn't true. It didn't cause me any anguish or agony. Remember at that time not all buildings were searched before the parade.

At a press conference on the evening of the bomb, the then Chief Constable of the RUC, Sir John Hermon, was asked why the building had not been searched. He replied that it simply was not considered a risk because it was known that only civilians stood there. The matter was taken up by the Member of Parliament for the area, Ulster Unionist Ken Maginnis. He wrote to the Chief Constable, again posing the question. A chief superintendent, on behalf of Sir John Hermon, replied:

I must emphasise that no influence whatsoever was brought to bear on the Royal Ulster Constabulary in this connection.

Given its location as a gathering point for members of the public attending the Remembrance ceremony it was not conceivable that terrorists would perpetrate such an appalling atrocity against the population. I am informed also that the building had not been searched in previous years either.

Before 1987, it would indeed have been thought unlikely that the IRA would attack a group of civilians at a Remembrance Day event. An attack on such a ceremony, with hundreds of civilians present, was unprecedented.

In security terms, what made the ceremony a high-risk event was the participation of groups of Crown forces. RUC men would be on duty in a non-terrorist policing capacity, and the main body of the parade in Enniskillen contained a column of 115 men and women from the Ulster Defence Regiment in army dress uniform. Years ago, these soldiers used to parade through Enniskillen from their base on the outskirts of town, to take their place at the War Memorial. But as fears of ambush had grown, the authorities had stopped this practice and the soldiers were transported to a car park off a side street, from where they marched a shorter distance to the cenotaph. Afterwards, they paraded through the town centre to a service of remembrance. The security risk, therefore, was thought to be in the areas where they would be. Any advance security precautions were focused there.

Although soldiers and policemen co-operated in checking the area in advance with sniffer dogs, the security plan for 1987 was the responsibility of high-ranking RUC officers in Enniskillen. In addition to keeping a discreet watch on traffic through the area, searches were made on Saturday evening and Sunday morning, including checking doorways along the parade route and, more thoroughly, inside certain buildings. A senior RUC officer decided that the Reading Rooms should not be searched.

On the Sunday morning, just after eight o'clock, there was a final security sweep of the area. One theory is that the soldiers conducting this final check were the real target of the bombers. However, the search did not take in the interior of the Reading Rooms where the bomb was in place.

In the circumstances of the time and in view of the fact that no such attack had ever occurred before, the level of advance security was considered reasonable. While it is highly unlikely that the Catholic Church authorities would formally object to any search, it is also true that in the very sensitive circumstances in Northern Ireland, the RUC would not have wanted to appear heavy-handed when dealing with the Catholic Church.

It was only with hindsight that so much was made of the decision not to search. The man who made that decision has now retired from the RUC, and declined a request for an interview. His colleagues maintain the official RUC line of the past ten years: the building was not considered a risk because only civilians stood there.

Significance of Remembrance Sunday

It was precisely because only civilians stood in that place that the IRA came in for so much criticism. Many of the families of those killed find it difficult to accept the IRA's explanation that their loved ones were killed by mistake. Is it possible that the IRA's mistake was not appreciating the very nature of the occasion, seeing it only as a British military event attended by those who support the British armed forces?

Remembrance Sunday is a very important day in the emotional psyche of the Unionist tradition. A measure of just how much it means can be gauged from the fact that sales of the poppy each year in Northern Ireland are usually the highest of all regions in the United Kingdom.

Poppies go on sale a few weeks before Remembrance Sunday each year, and throughout Britain millions of pounds have been raised for the Royal British Legion's work in helping the families of servicemen and women killed in wars, as well as those disabled in recent wars such as the Gulf and the Falklands conflicts. One year in the 1980s, the town of Enniskillen sold over £15,000 worth of poppies, the highest of any Royal British Legion branch throughout the United Kingdom. Remarkably, this average of 40p per head of population is almost double the British average. When one considers that most Nationalists do not buy the poppy, it shows how the Unionist community responds.

Those attending the ceremony at the War Memorial in Enniskillen pay tribute to men and women killed in war. But they are not just honouring people from history. Many of those standing in silence year after year have personal reasons for being there: they are remembering members of their own families who served, and in many cases died, on foreign fields.

Sammy Foster, who has attended as a member of Fermanagh District Council in recent years, started going to the ceremony in 1953 when he first moved to Enniskillen. He says:

> I would say the vast majority of people there had somebody who served in the forces, whether in the First World War or Second World War. My wife and I both have family who died named on the Memorial. My father's family served in the Great War and my mother's younger brother, named Johnston, died at the Somme.

Mr Foster remembers his cousin, Raymond Toland, being at the family home in 1944, a fortnight before he went on a bombing mission over France. He never returned.

Alberta Quinton, one of the victims of the bomb, served in the Women's Royal Air Force. She always wore her medals to the Enniskillen ceremony, which was important to her as a way of honouring her colleagues who did not return.

Sam Murray helped with the rescue at Enniskillen. His father had the distinction of fighting and being wounded in both world wars, having first joined the British Army in the First World War at the age of just 12 years and 9 months. Sam says:

> He lied about his age to go. He was a big lad so he got away with it. He went to France and was wounded. Even though he was banned from joining up again when they found out about his age, as soon as he was better he went away to Scotland and joined the Seaforth Highlanders.

Mr Murray's father was called up again in 1939 and fought again in the Second World War until he was wounded in 1942.

Sam Murray's wife, Phyllis, was also at the War Memorial honouring, among others, her father, Tommy Elliott from Florencecourt. He was gassed at the Somme, but survived to live to the age of 83. Mr Murray says: 'It was always important that we went on account of them.'

Many others who attend have similar personal reasons for being there. A large number of children from schools and youth organisations also attend, having heard stories of their grandparents' part in the war. At the other end of the age scale, 'old soldiers' remember their own service. For example, Ballyreagh bandsman Freddie Miller served in the Royal Inniskilling Fusiliers.

Military History

Fermanagh has a strong military history. The town of Enniskillen was the only town in the British Isles to 'raise' two regiments, one infantry and one cavalry. The Royal Inniskilling Fusiliers and the Royal Inniskilling Dragoons were formed in the town over 300 years ago. British Government cutbacks in the past twenty years have meant that a number of regiments have been amalgamated, and the Inniskilling name — the old spelling of Enniskillen — does not exist in today's army. But both regiments had become famous over the years, with numerous battle honours to their credit, and reputations for producing stubborn fighting men.

The 27th Inniskilling Regiment of Foot was the only

Irish infantry regiment to fight Napoleon at Waterloo in 1815. Regimental legend has it that Napoleon said:

> That regiment with the castles on their caps is composed of the most obstinate mules I ever saw; they don't know when they are beaten.

The Dragoons, too, have a distinguished history. Among their officers was Captain Lawrence Oates, who was on Scott's expedition to the Antarctic in 1912. As conditions worsened and rations reached a low point, he sacrificed his life for others by walking out of the tent into a blizzard, telling colleagues that he might be gone for some time. A plaque in his memory in the hallway of Enniskillen Townhall quotes John Masefield on Oates, saying:

> Knowing the storm without, the dwindling food,
> His failing strength, his comrades' constancy,
> This man, in hope to save them, thought it good,
> To walk alone into the snow to die.

Soldiers from the 'Skins', as the regiments are nick-named, fought in the two world wars. The Fusiliers were in the 36th Ulster Division, which lost thousands at the Battle of the Somme in 1916.

A feature of both regiments is that large numbers of men from their original home — both Protestants and Catholics — continued to serve throughout this century.

War Memorial

A sign of Enniskillen's strong military link is the War Memorial itself, built in 1922. An impressive bronze statue of a soldier with head bowed was built on a stone base. It is a more distinguished memorial than many in larger towns and cities throughout Britain. A plaque has been on the memorial from the beginning, bearing the names of 622 men from Fermanagh killed in the First World War. Over 300 of them are from the Royal Inniskilling Fusiliers, both officers and men. The list of names reflects the fact that men from both communities served and died. From the Protestant tradition, there are common Fermanagh names, such as Johnston, Wilson and Armstrong. Catholic family names include Maguire, Gallagher, Keenan and McManus.

In 1995, fifty years after the end of the Second World War, another list was added to the memorial, with the names of 214 Fermanagh people who died in that war.

The Religious Divide

Clearly, there is a tradition of serving in the British Army which transcends the religious divide. However, in Northern Ireland, Remembrance Day has come to be more closely associated with the Protestant–Unionist tradition, and men who fought together and watched their comrades die fighting the common enemies of the Kaiser and Hitler now feel unable to pay homage together. All eleven people killed at Enniskillen were Protestants.

Attitudes to Remembrance Day illustrate how perceptions increase the sense of two communities in Northern Ireland. The First World War took place before the Partition of Ireland and many Catholics from throughout Ireland served in the British Army. It was more common for Catholics to attend the Remembrance Day ceremony up until the 1930s. However, as the century progressed many Catholics began to feel uneasy about attending, the perception having grown that Remembrance Day is an occasion for Unionists. In Northern Ireland, the term 'Protestant' has come to be taken to imply 'Unionist', while 'Catholic' is taken to mean 'Nationalist'.

In recent years, there have been moves from certain quarters in the Republic of Ireland to have greater recognition of Remembrance Day. Supporters point out that tens of thousands of Irishmen, such as those from the Dublin Fusiliers, fought and were killed in the First World War and should be honoured. However, there is still considerable debate as to how this should be done, and there are many shades of opinion throughout the island. Staunch Republicans, for example, would feel that anything done in paying homage to Irishmen who fought with the British would give credence and respectability to a hated, foreign army. It would be anathema to them to honour what they would term British imperial militarism.

This view is at one end of the spectrum. In Northern Ireland, many Nationalists would simply feel uncomfortable at a ceremony with British connotations. While there are some Catholics who do go to pay homage to the dead, the majority of people at the ceremonies are Protestants.

While those Protestants would not regard being there as a great display of Britishness — they are simply honouring their dead at a simple ceremony, which is also a solemn, religious occasion — it is difficult for many of them to accept that the IRA bombing was anything other than an attack on the Unionist community in general and their British way of life.

Who was the Target?

The Unionist MP for Fermanagh–South Tyrone, Ken Maginnis, 'absolutely and totally' dismisses the IRA claim that its members made a mistake:

> There was never any question but that civilians would be standing on the footpath. They stood there every year. I have no doubt that it was deliberately aimed at the Protestant population; it was civilian Protestants that were being targeted. The idea that you would have lots of soldiers or policemen on the footpath is nonsense, not that the crime would have been any less dreadful. Anybody, Protestant or Catholic, Unionist or Republican, who knows the area would understand fully that what the IRA are saying by way of explanation is a downright lie.

He also disagrees with the theory that attacking civilians would have been a change of tactic for the IRA:

> I never cease to be amazed that after twenty-seven to thirty years, people still do not understand fully the nature of terrorism. Terrorism is what the word suggests, it is something that is intended to terrorise the civilian community into submission. It is not about killing

soldiers or policemen — that is simply a means to an end. It is about terrorising the civilian population so that they will capitulate. Look at the numbers who have been killed: the large majority are civilians. Loyalist terrorism is no different. Loyalists have by and large killed innocent members of the Catholic community.

Another Ulster Unionist, Fermanagh Councillor Raymond Ferguson believes that the IRA did not care who was killed that day:

If they were after UDR soldiers, in my own view that is just as heinous. They like to justify their actions, but I think the overall policy is to cause as much mayhem as possible. In Republican thinking, this is an event that shouldn't be held anyway because it was a foreign ceremony. The Republican philosophy that can justify that is one I certainly can't empathise with; I suppose there is a logic to it, but certainly none you could give any credit to.

It is a cheap culture that says we must get our way, we don't care what the consequences are because what we are aiming for is justified.

Councillor Sammy Foster is unsure what the IRA target was on 8 November 1987:

Whether it was what they intended, only they themselves know. I feel they did not want it to go off at that stage. My opinion is that it went wrong. Perhaps it was intended to go off should anybody be searching the Reading Rooms or go off afterwards as a protest against a British-orientated event. These are only assumptions of mine, I have no evidence. But whatever their intention, I wouldn't be giving them any credibility because that day they did murder.

It is not inconceivable that the 115 UDR men and women on parade in Enniskillen were a target, and there is no doubt that this is what the soldiers of the UDR themselves believe. Some even say privately that they noticed a reluctance by some members of the Protestant community to associate with them in the days after the bombing, implying a perverse sort of blame for the deaths.

The Ulster Defence Regiment was formed after the

disbandment of the B Specials in 1971, with many of their soldiers serving part-time. They became a prime target for the IRA and, in Fermanagh alone, twenty-five UDR men were killed — either blown up by booby-trap bombs or shot dead in ambushes. The UDR has now been amalgamated into the Royal Irish Regiment,

Tullyhommon

In speculating on the IRA's real intention, many people repeatedly remind you, 'Don't forget Tullyhommon.'

On the same day as the Enniskillen bomb, another bomb had been placed close to where the Remembrance Sunday ceremony was taking place at Tullyhommon, about fifteen miles from Enniskillen on the Fermanagh–Donegal Border. Tullyhommon is the 'northern half' of Pettigo, with the two straddling the Border. The majority of people taking part were young people — almost 200 from the local Boys Brigade and Girls Brigade organisations. Along with adults, they laid their wreaths and then headed for church, completely unaware that a 200-pound land mine packed into metal drums was sitting yards away beside the local cattle pens.

A command wire from the bomb led to a point in a field across the Border in Co. Donegal, but it had failed to detonate. Nobody even knew that the bomb was there until almost five o'clock that afternoon when a call was made to the Downtown Radio newsroom in Newtownards.

The then head of news, David Sloan, recalls answering an operator who told him that there was a call from Donegal. By this time, the station had spent a busy afternoon broadcasting news of the Enniskillen atrocity. When the Donegal caller claimed to be from the West Fermanagh Brigade of the IRA, David Sloan assumed that the IRA was admitting responsibility for Enniskillen. To his surprise, the caller warned of the danger of a bomb at Tullyhommon. A senior police officer and an army officer had been standing close to the bomb that morning. The caller said: 'When I pushed the button, nothing happened.'

David listened to the warning that the bomb was still live and a danger to passers-by, and then asked the IRA man, 'What about Enniskillen?'

The caller replied, 'That's nothing to do with us, Boss. South Fermanagh will probably be on to you.'

Tullyhommon was immediately sealed off and the bomb was found. Security forces in Donegal were contacted and they found the ignition point. Plastic connectors in the command wire had not been fitted properly, and the connection had not been made. The bomb was made safe.

In an interview published in Enniskillen's *Impartial Reporter* on 7 January 1988, Boys Brigade captain in the area Mervyn Rowe said that people on parade knew nothing about the bomb until they heard it on the radio on Sunday evening:

> It was only then that the real horror of what might have happened hit us. For those first few hours, there was a real sense of shock through the community. If the bomb had gone off, it would have wiped out the young Protestant people for a six-mile radius.

Ken Maginnis also refers to this incident:

> It is often forgotten that on the same day as the slaughter took place in Enniskillen, a bomb was planted at Tullyhommon which was intended to wipe out the youth of that area. They can't say they thought it was going to be a lot of soldiers they killed there. When one writes up Enniskillen, it mustn't be forgotten that Tullyhommon was designed to wipe out a whole generation of young people who were assembling for a similar parade.

After the Remembrance Sunday massacre, there were some changes to security. More than 500 extra British troops were brought in, and a 'Border zone' was created where tighter security measures were operated. Yet, because of the geographical nature of the area, the heavy security measures could only ever be a containment. Whatever the target in 1987, the IRA campaign of bombings and shootings continued.

7: The Spirit of Enniskillen

The message to come out of Enniskillen in the days and weeks following the bomb was that the community at large, and families of victims in particular, were very forgiving. The tone was set by Gordon Wilson's interview on Sunday evening when he said that he bore no grudge and that he would pray for the killers of his daughter, Marie.

In another interview, not given as much publicity as Gordon Wilson's, the brother of another victim spoke of his hopes for reconciliation. Methodist Minister, the Rev. Bertie Armstrong, whose brother Wesley was killed, said:

> Those of us who tried to keep the message of repentance, forgiveness and reconciliation at the centre of our suffering have been greatly encouraged.

With the passage of time, though, it has become clear that many other reactions have not been given a full airing. Among the bereaved families, the injured and others in Enniskillen there has been a variety of responses. Indeed, on reflection, it would seem improbable that an entire community should react in the same way. At the time, many people were either too numb with shock to express how they really felt, or they submerged their feeling for fear of betraying the image of forgiveness that the media had built up. The fact that some could not quite identify with Gordon Wilson's words of forgiveness did not mean that they were at the other extreme either. There was a range of emotions in between.

Not unexpectedly, in the volatile hours after the bombing there were little bursts of fury from some individuals. Unionist Councillor Raymond Ferguson recalls that in the immediate moments after the bomb, one Catholic man who had attended the ceremony was picked on by a few people:

> I felt sorry for him. Because of the anger and the horror of the thing, it wasn't unnatural for people to start looking for scapegoats. They became a bit irate and started shouting that it was his people who had done this. But he was saying he had nothing to do with it. It was only one small incident.

Another Catholic at the cenotaph was the Chief Executive of Fermanagh District Council, Gerry Burns, who remembers a man coming up to him and expressing anti-Catholic sentiments:

> I know him and respected him as a good man. He later apologised and I quite understood his attitude in the heat of the moment.

One Protestant who had been involved in the rescue was later heard to go into the Royal British Legion hall and castigate the bombers as 'Fenian bastards'. The Legion has both Protestant and Catholic members, and the few who heard his remark passed it off.

The Presbyterian minister, the Rev. David Cupples, recalls going into his church hall when news was coming through that six of his congregation had died:

> There was one man I remember talking to. I lifted my hands out in bewilderment. He responded with an outburst saying we have been holding our hands up for far too long; somebody ought to go up and blow up the chapel.

These incidents, regrettable as they were, tended to be isolated and were put down to hot-headedness. While there has been some history within Fermanagh of Loyalist paramilitary activity, Loyalist terror organisations have never had much strength in the county. However, in the wider Northern Ireland context, the UDA, UFF and UVF would be likely to regard the attack on Enniskillen as an attack on Loyalism and Protestantism generally. At the back of many minds in the security forces was the fear of a backlash and the expectation that Loyalist paramilitaries might exact grim revenge by killing Catholics.

However, Gordon Wilson's interview, and the widespread response to it, removed any justification the Loyalists may have found. To have killed ordinary Catholics in revenge for the death of Marie Wilson would have been regarded as grotesque.

Neither would the other bereaved families have wanted to see any backlash against their Catholic neighbours, although some of them could not quite grasp how Gordon Wilson could be seen to be forgiving the IRA.

Forgiveness

James Mullan sums up the feelings of many bereaved relatives, regarding Gordon Wilson's interview:

> I initially was very sceptical of what he said. I know he was talking personally — he wasn't talking for me or the rest of the families. But I thought it was beyond my comprehension, I couldn't have done what he did. There was some contact between the other families; some people asked me how I felt. There was one family who were so annoyed that they wanted to make it known that they didn't agree with what he said. But my attitude was that we should sit back and say nothing. If anything good would come out of what he said it would be worthwhile . . . I said in all fairness we can't rewrite history, but at least the tragedy is making people listen to what we are going through. We were not unique: boys that sat in the same class as me at Portora Royal School subsequently joined the RUC and were murdered. Neighbours of mine in the police were blown to pieces. People in England in particular were fed up listening to atrocity after atrocity, and the people here as a community were becoming used to it. So, at least they were listening to us now. But I could understand some of the reaction by the families to what Gordon Wilson was saying.

Other relatives shrug their shoulders when asked about forgiveness. They simply do not feel that they can express it. Joe Kennedy, whose wife, Ruth, lost her parents, Kit and Jessie Johnston, says:

> Don't ask me about forgiveness — it's not relevant. I believe there is no forgiveness without repentance. If you brought some person along who said, 'We did it. We are sorry. Will you forgive us?' we might start to think about it.

Gladys Gault's view on forgiving the killers of her husband, Sammy, is:

> I don't think it is up to us. In time, God will deal with those people. I wouldn't want vengeance or retaliation, but I don't think it is up to me to judge on forgiveness.

Aileen Quinton was annoyed to hear that Cardinal Tomás Ó Fiaich had apologised on behalf of the Catholic people:

> That was a stupid thing to do because the only people in a position to apologise for it are the IRA and the people who support them.

She had no objections to Gordon Wilson's original interview:

> He never said he forgave. Has everybody else started saying that? To me it is morally indefensible to forgive people who aren't sorry.

The subject of forgiveness was much debated after Enniskillen, and Rev. David Cupples felt that he should address it. He preached a sermon on the subject to his congregation five weeks after the bombing. He says:

> There is the widely held assumption that when you say you forgive, you are saying that what was done didn't really matter. That is certainly not what people intend to say. The debate also rages in the Christian Church about whether you can forgive people before they repent. I believe if we are to follow the example of Jesus, we must offer forgiveness unconditionally. But the person who has committed the injury cannot actually have an experience

of forgiveness unless they admit they have done something wrong.

Anger

While many in Enniskillen, whether directly or indirectly affected, could not bring themselves to address the subject of forgiveness, many other legitimate emotions were evident. Rev. Cupples says:

> There were very few expressions of anger, but there is absolutely no question that it was there. It was inevitable, but it was righteous anger. I think people are under the false impression that anger is an entirely wrong and unhealthy emotion. But I think there are a lot of things in this world that we ought to be angry about. Enniskillen was certainly one of them. The danger is that because we are fallible people, our anger can be tinged with all sorts of wrong motives. But there can still be some righteous and proper anger when we see monstrous evil perpetrators and innocent people as their victims.
>
> Of course people were outraged, but there is a sort of basic decency about the kind of folk I deal with in Fermanagh. No matter how angry they were, they were not the kind of people who were likely to take the law into their own hands.

Councillor Raymond Ferguson says that there was bound to be anger when the enormity of the atrocity became clear:

> It was the most atrocious event to date that happened in the IRA campaign. There is no doubt there was huge anger. Gordon Wilson was the focus of a lot of forgiveness and Christian turning the other cheek. But in the Protestant community generally there was a lot of anger about it. People were bewildered and they were angry, and there is still a residue of anger about it. It is naïve to think that you can make a strike against a community as pointedly as that and not leave any residue of anger. There was disbelief as well.

Many of these feelings of anger were expressed privately. Some months after the bomb, private meetings were held to help the bereaved and injured, and at one such gathering, local man John Maxwell was invited to speak. He has personal experience of loss as a result of terrorism: his 15-year-old son, Paul, was killed when the IRA blew up Lord Mountbatten's boat at Mullaghmore in 1979.

John Maxwell has a long and remarkable history of words and actions of reconciliation. At one point during his address, he said that it was sometimes helpful if the Troubles were seen in their historical context. However, on this occasion, his words were misunderstood by some, and there was a reaction by a few against what he was saying. For many of those present, it was just too early in their rehabilitation. They had not reached the point where they could transcend their anger.

The Church of Ireland rector, Canon John McCarthy, understands the feelings of bitterness among his congregation:

> It must be terribly difficult for those people who had relatives murdered not to feel embittered in some way and certainly to feel that those responsible should be brought to justice. It wasn't a case of forgive and forget. It was such a dastardly thing. People had suffered. There was forgiveness in the right sense, but not that these people should walk free from the whole thing. I think there was a tremendous amount of dignity though.
>
> But there was great pain too. I can understand ten years later how people who have suffered wonder about IRA and Sinn Féin talking about the challenge of bringing peace. Yet nobody has said sorry for Enniskillen. The pain must still be there for the victims.

According to Raymond Ferguson, by and large, the feelings of anger were directed at Sinn Féin, although not always:

> Those directly affected had an understandable anger about the loss they had suffered. Sometimes when you are in that mood, you are not fully focused on who you are trying to identify. So sometimes bitterness didn't just stop at Sinn Féin.

While the debate on forgiveness can become bogged down in theological discussion, the fact remains that some people in Enniskillen are still annoyed that there has been no apology. In a sermon on injustice, the Rev. Cupples referred to the twenty-fifth anniversary of Bloody Sunday, when British Paratroopers shot dead thirteen civilians (a fourteenth man died later as a result of his injuries). Rev. Cupples recalls:

> Someone in the church said, 'There is always fury about Bloody Sunday, but they haven't got anyone for Enniskillen.' What was coming through was the feeling that the people who died here didn't matter as much because there isn't the same fuss made about it.

The attack on Enniskillen was a particularly brutal one. Whatever the intention, the result was that innocent people were slaughtered, bodies were broken and individuals were left to cope with an awful situation. The fact that the anger and hurt have not always been expressed in a vitriolic way does not mean that they have not been there. Nor is it remarkable that ten years on they are still there. What is remarkable is that the people of Enniskillen responded with such dignity, and actually came closer together rather than being driven further apart.

Perhaps this is the real spirit of Enniskillen: a courageous and dignified community that has its differences but refuses to let actions, however evil, deflect them from what they know to be right.

The Fundamentalist Spirit

The hope for reconciliation between Protestants and Catholics was not held by everyone. Some fundamentalists believed that Protestants should be warned about the dangers of ecumenism. The Rev. Ivan Foster, a minister in the Free Presbyterian Church, published a four-page leaflet on the aftermath of Enniskillen, and distributed it around homes in the area. Some members of his congregation had been injured in the bomb. He described his publication as 'The Untold Story'. In one section, Rev. Foster writes:

> I do believe the clerics have gone too far and the attempts at promoting unity through the grief caused by this massacre is [*sic*] beginning to sicken Protestants. 'It is not good to eat much honey,' say the Scriptures. It is certainly so with ecumenical honey. Rome has quietly and surreptitiously encouraged the Enniskillen ecumenists.

Rev. Foster also criticised the holding of a special Mass in St Michael's Roman Catholic church to pray for the victims. He said:

> It is difficult for evangelical Protestants in Co. Fermanagh to take in the effrontery of Rome in organising a mass for the repose of the soul of Johnny Megaw, Sam Gault and the other believers who were murdered.

The minister gave an explanation of why he was opposed to any link with the Catholic Church and added:

> The cup of ecumenism is being pressed urgently to the lips of the Protestant community. I appeal to all Protestants before they drink and consequently lose all ability to grasp what is taking place that they heed God's word.

In addition to criticism of those speaking in favour of reconciliation, including ecumenical Protestant clergymen, Rev. Foster printed in full a letter that he had sent to me, as Editor of *The Impartial Reporter*, the local newspaper in Enniskillen. I had refused to publish it.

His letter read:

> Much has been said about the Enniskillen massacre. Strong words of condemnation have been quite rightly used. Sadly, an examination of many of the statements shows a total lack of understanding of what it is that the Ulster Protestant is facing. The whole tragic affair could have been avoided had the premises containing the bomb been properly searched before the parade. The bitter anti-police feelings within the Roman Catholic Church, which in past years showed itself [*sic*] whenever the building was searched before the Remembrance Day ceremony,

caused senior police officers to forgo the search this year.

The decision not to search the building is an example of the continual capitulation to Roman Catholic Nationalism which has enabled the IRA campaign to continue until now. Effective measures against the terrorists are curtailed because it would bring a storm of protest from the Roman Catholic Church. Consequently, Protestants must live and die with tragedies like Sunday past. It is forgivable, therefore, if a person views a little sceptically the sympathy of those who in different circumstances would have been crying police harassment.

As a gospel minister who longs to see this country return to the paths of true Biblical righteousness, I have watched with grieved heart the exploitation of this terrible tragedy by the ecumenical clerics in Enniskillen. That which should be used to turn the people back to the God of the Holy Scriptures is instead being used to advance unity with Romanism. Is it not ironic that the Church of Rome, whose intransigence and anti-police feelings are largely to blame for the bomb not being detected, should now be a trustee of the fund established to help the victims of the bombing?

Surely Enniskillen Protestants are not so deceived as to not see this deceit. The fact that Mrs Thatcher is to be brought to Enniskillen further emphasises this deception. Can the grieving and injured from the bombing be comforted by a Prime Minister whose policy has been one of totally ignoring the community which was bombed and who is actively engaged with Dublin in subverting the constitutional rights of that same people?

My prayer is that the message of the terrible events of Sunday 8th November will indeed prove to be a catalyst, as referred to by the Bishop of Clogher, but unlike him I wish to see the people turn to the God of the Bible and not to the false god of ecumenism. Let every one who fears God read Amos 4: 6–13 and heed the message of the bombing.

In his private publication, Rev. Foster pointed out that *The Impartial Reporter* had refused to publish his letter and said: 'The ecumenical spirit is never very partial to hard truth.'

Throughout my ten years as Editor, I have rarely re-fused to publish authenticated letters in the paper, except on legal grounds or because of lack of space. My difficulties with the above letter were that in it Rev. Foster was making unsubstantiated claims about the alleged failure to search the building; he was attacking the Catholic Church in general and one individual in particu-lar at a time when there was a highly charged atmo-sphere; he was also attacking the faith of a particular Protestant clergyman at a very sensitive time.

Among the things I had to consider was whether such a contribution and the way it was worded would inflame the situation. My gut instinct was that Ivan Foster's letter just was not right in the circumstances, and I went with my instinct even though it left me open to accusations of censorship. I was grateful at the time for the support of my friend and former mentor, Mervyn Dane.

Ivan Foster and I continued on first-name terms, al-though he took every opportunity to let me know in no uncertain manner what he perceived to be the error of my ways. Such strong views as his were not altogether iso-lated. In some quarters, mistrust deepened and divisions were accentuated after the bombing. On a plaque un-veiled in memory of Johnny Megaw, the Democratic Unionist party's inscription read that he was 'murdered by the Roman Catholic IRA'.

One of the people seriously injured in the Enniskillen bomb is an outspoken critic of the Catholic Church. Jim Dixon's view is that the Catholic Church in Europe has been guilty of 'brutal massacre over 600 years'. He says, 'I am not antagonistic to ordinary Catholics, but I know what they belong to.' In a television interview after the bomb, he described the IRA as the 'military wing of the Catholic Church.'

A member of the Presbyterian Church, Jim Dixon was born and raised in Clones, Co. Monaghan. His family had businesses in Clones, Mullingar and Newtownbutler in Fermanagh. The Newtownbutler garage he owned was bombed by the IRA in the 1970s. He believes that this was part of a campaign against Protestants in the area:

> Everything is done against the Protestants. It is a plan of genocide but it didn't work out because Protestants didn't run from the Border.

When the then Northern Ireland Secretary of State, Tom King, visited Jim Dixon in hospital, the injured man accused the politician to his face of having 'hands dripping with the blood of the Protestants of Ulster'. Mr Dixon explains:

> He says, 'You are an angry man.' 'No,' I said; 'I am a righteous man full of righteous indignation, looking at a man that has a job to do and isn't doing it. The violence has to be destroyed. If you don't destroy them, they will destroy both you and the United Kingdom.'
> The media tried to tell me that I was bitter. I wasn't the slightest bit bitter. I am a man that lives on facts and deals with them. I believe in the law of the country and anyone that tries to destroy that law should be executed straight away.

Mr Dixon's views were at the opposite end of the spectrum from those of Gordon Wilson. He says:

> It annoyed me badly to hear that he forgave the IRA. What right had he? It was obnoxious. They had committed a sin against humanity, not against him. They had committed a sin against God. Forgiveness has a criterion built into it. God never forgave an evil man, God only forgives a repenting man.

A number of people around Enniskillen also privately belittle Gordon Wilson's account of what happened under the rubble, but few feel comfortable speaking about such a delicate matter publicly.

The Media Affair

Gordon Wilson is such a widely respected figure across the world and did so much good that it may come as a surprise to many that there is some bad feeling towards him within his own county. Nevertheless there are those who felt that his high profile was unfair to other victims who seemed to be forgotten. One relative described Mr Wilson's relationship with the media as 'the affair'.

In general though, there was widespread support for Gordon Wilson in Fermanagh. He often sounded out people before taking particular actions, although clearly he was a determined man who felt his mission in life was to make efforts for peace. Social worker David Bolton, who formed a close relationship with him and with whom he would discuss controversial matters, pays tribute:

> I came to admire him enormously. The work he was doing was amazing and maybe we will never know the half of it. I think he was doing things that we may never read about until the thirty-year government embargo is over. I know he has come in for a lot of criticism and I know he wasn't a perfect man. But if you look at it from the point of view of where we all stand on the day of judgment before God, I think Gordon Wilson has a good story to tell. The Old Testament prophets stood out in protest against the way the world was and pointed a different way forward.
>
> I think that is what Gordon Wilson did. Maybe as a community we lose sight of the good that he was doing; in that sense he was a prophet without honour in his own country. When I saw him in the Dublin Forum for Peace and Reconciliation, railing at Sinn Féin and others who said things he didn't approve of, one couldn't help but be greatly impressed with his courage, strength and clarity.

There was some opposition to Mr Wilson's acceptance of a seat in the Irish Senate. He knew that there would be opposition, but among the factors which persuaded him to take up the position was the belief that his presence would be a constant public reminder of what had happened at Enniskillen. There was also opposition to his meeting with the IRA. When Gordon Wilson died in 1995, there were no official representatives from the Unionist parties at his funeral, although some Unionist friends did attend in a personal capacity. Although there was division over Gordon Wilson's role, it is important to emphasise that the strand of opinion which was opposed to the coming together of the two communities, was a minority one and in the weeks following the bomb, what came to be known as the 'spirit of Enniskillen' shone around the world.

Appeal Fund

The positive way in which the Enniskillen community responded struck a chord with people worldwide who were horrified by what had happened. This resulted in a phenomenal response to the appeal fund set up by Gerry Burns. He says:

> One was always very conscious that Enniskillen was a community that had a very strong central core of understanding and friendly people. They responded in a beautiful and dignified way. In the end it was a community I was very proud to be part of.

As a Catholic in a prominent public position in the county, Gerry Burns felt that he should take on a leading role:

> My role was really one that focused on the community at large and where we were all going. I was a step removed from the actual personal grief and hurt felt by individuals.

Mr Burns worked as treasurer of the appeal fund in a personal capacity. He praises the work done by the four churchmen after the bomb.

Church of Ireland rector, Canon John McCarthy, and Presbyterian minister, the Rev. David Cupples, had known each other before coming to Enniskillen, having played hockey together for Banbridge. Monsignor Seán Cahill, was originally from Co. Monaghan. Moving across the border in 1981 had for the first time brought him face to face with the sensitivities of a divided society. Making up the quartet was the tall, older Methodist minister, the Rev. Tom Magowan.

In spite of differences in background, personality and theological outlook, they got on famously and worked well together at a crucial time in the town's history. Along with the other trustees, they were responsible for administering the £660,000 that arrived from all corners of the globe. Gerry Burns says:

> It is easy enough collecting money, would you believe? It is more difficult distributing it and therefore a great deal of work had to be done.

Having sought advice from places such as Bradford and Hungerford, where disaster funds had been set up, Enniskillen formed two trusts — alongside the appeal fund there was a charitable trust which technically made the pay-outs.

The trustees decided at an early stage that at least 80 per cent would go to those directly affected, namely the bereaved and injured. They published their initial aims:

> 1. The priority is to tend to the needs of the bereaved, the injured and their families.
>
> 2. We recognise that there is a wish within the community to have some form of permanent memorial.

To cope with the first part, Gerry Burns suggested that a social worker should be appointed to link with the families. He felt that Sammy Foster would be the person most suited: 'People would talk to him because they knew him and respected him.'

Sammy Foster, an Ulster Unionist member of Fermanagh District Council, was seconded from his job with social services. He was in a unique position, having been at the War Memorial when the bomb went off. Having almost become a victim himself, he was once again helping those who actually had.

Mr Foster became engaged in a lengthy process, making personal contact with a total of 134 people. His role was a mixture of listening, counselling and form-filling. He spoke with twenty-nine members of the eight families who had had somebody killed; the remainder were people injured or traumatised on the day. A form asking thirty questions was completed on subjects ranging from their feelings, to financial and material loss.

Mr Foster found a range of emotions:

> a profound sense of desolation, shock, brooding, anger, resentment, recurring waves of depression, feeling bereft and alone, severe anxiety and tremendous faith.

The answers were assessed by a panel, comprising a local businessman, a psychiatrist and a surgeon. Some initial payments were made to cover things like funeral expenses, but after the lengthy assessment process had been completed, £579,974 — over 90 per cent of the amount originally collected — was distributed. Legal steps were taken to ensure that any payment received would not affect any other compensation that victims would receive, and would be exempt from income tax.

The payments to each of the 134 individuals remained confidential, but they ranged from about £400 to one payment of £50,000. The money, while not a fortune, was intended to help people over their practical difficulties.

While allocating money is always open to criticism, there was little dispute about the way it was handled in this case, and it was generally felt that the cash went to where the people who donated it would have intended.

New Memorial

The second part of the trustees' brief, to provide a memorial, proved rather more difficult. It became clear that a consensus on the venue and type of memorial would be difficult to achieve. The trustees faced the difficulty of matching the opposition of some of the families with what the wider community felt was acceptable.

Several sites were considered around the town. They included the Diamond area in the town centre and Castle Island near the Broadmeadow recreation grounds. However, it was thought more appropriate that something should be done, either where the bomb had exploded or at least in the area of the cenotaph. Mr Burns says:

> It was felt that as the Remembrance ceremony was held at the cenotaph, something should be done there.

At first, a garden of remembrance was proposed for the bomb site, which is the property of the Catholic Church. Monsignor Seán Cahill explains the difficulties in this.

Firstly, any plan to put a new building on the site, or indeed to landscape it, would meet with practical difficulties. The old Reading Rooms demolished in the blast were built well over a hundred years ago on the shore of the River Erne, and there is a steep drop down from the pavement to the bottom floors of the remains of the building. It is an awkward site, and estimates for putting a new structure in place range from £0.75 million to £1 million. The compensation offered was only £170,000.

Monsignor Cahill explains that the Church simply could not afford to pay for this out of St Michael's parish funds. While there has recently been a major renovation scheme at St Michael's church, he points out that it was something that had been in the pipeline for a long time.

Instead, local architect Richard Pierce was asked to come up with a design for a memorial at the cenotaph itself. When considering what form the tribute to the eleven victims should take, Mr Pierce wrote to the trustees:

> The existing memorial, the bronze soldier on a plinth, is already a memorial, in that it was the image used by the media all over the world as the visual focus. The bomb turned that bronze soldier from a provincial war memorial in a west Ulster market town into an international symbol of the triumph of ordinary decent people over cold-blooded terrorism.

Before the bomb, the Roads Service had considered re-siting the Memorial away from the middle of Belmore Street, which had seen a massive increase in traffic. After the bomb, any thoughts of moving were abandoned.

The existing War Memorial was redesigned and rebuilt

at a cost of £100,000. The bronze soldier on its Portland stone base was retained but the structure was raised on a higher stone base. Eleven bronze doves, sculpted by Philip Flanagan to represent each of the victims, were added. A bronze plaque was also added, with the inscription: 'In remembrance of 11 of our neighbours who were killed in a terrorist bomb at this site. . . .' The names of the victims were listed. The redesigned memorial was in place for Remembrance Day in 1991, when a short ceremony was held before the main act of remembrance.

The changes were not universally welcomed. Some felt that the new memorial was not aesthetically as pleasing as the old one and that the plaques were badly placed, making it difficult for people to read. However, the main objections concerned the use of the doves (symbols of peace) and the wording of the inscription.

Derek Quinton told the Trustees that using the word 'killed' instead of 'murdered' was downgrading the atrocity which had claimed his mother. His sister, Aileen, says that she finds it offensive when 'people play down the truth':

> The most important aspect is to reinforce and clarify that it was murder. If the trustees felt they couldn't cope with the word 'murder', then they should have given us the chance of veto. Nobody has ever asked our family for permission to put my mother's name on it or to have her represented by a creature. I think everybody has an obligation to show up terrorism and evil for what it is; don't pussy foot or pretend around it.

The trustees had given some thought to the wording. They were told that Gordon Wilson objected to the use of the term 'murdered'. Canon McCarthy admits that he was surprised at the time:

> I think those people were murdered; but there were some who felt strongly that the word shouldn't be used.

Rev. David Cupples explains that he personally has no hesitation in saying that the people were murdered:

Morally that is what happened. But when you have it set
in stone and in memorials it seems to have an emotive
connotation of anger and bitterness that I think should
not be conveyed. I think when it was stated that they
were killed by an IRA bomb, then it is perfectly clear what
the facts of the matter are and people can make their
simple moral judgment.

There were obviously relatives who wanted the word
'murdered' to appear, but there was also one family who
said if the word 'murdered' appeared, their relative's
name could not go on it.

The Presbyterian Church later commissioned a beautiful
stained-glass window in memory of the members of their
congregation who lost their lives in the bombing. It also
refers to their being 'killed by an IRA bomb'.

The Enniskillen memorial is unique in that it is the
only war memorial in the United Kingdom which bears
the names of civilians. All the others commemorate members of the forces killed in action. Perhaps more than the
wording, the fact of the memorial being rebuilt at all was
a cause of displeasure. Aileen Quinton says:

I have two problems with it. I have a problem with the
fact that there were eleven of those creatures on the War
Memorial and therefore one of those is meant to represent
my mother. I think it is dreadful to have civilians on it: it
is a war memorial. She would not have liked that at all. It
was a lovely war memorial as it was and, to my mind,
they have vandalised it. If I pass it I would turn my head
the other way; I try to imagine and pretend to myself that
it hasn't been touched.

Another relative, James Mullan, was approached by a
large number of people objecting to the new design:

We felt that the War Memorial was a unit that should
have been left as it was. In all fairness, I ended up happy
enough with the wording, but I did not like this idea of
tampering with the existing War Memorial. I didn't
particularly like the idea of doves. I went to London that
summer when all this controversy was on and I stood

outside the war memorial at Whitehall. It was simple, no ornamentation. I thought I should bring the people from Enniskillen over to see it.

The Rev. Cupples explains that, as well as being symbols of peace, the eleven bronze doves also convey innocence, representing the innocence of those who died.

In 1992, one of these doves disappeared from the memorial. Gerry Burns believes that it was not a wanton piece of vandalism, but rather that the dove was taken by someone who recognised its artistic value. Neither the culprit nor the missing dove was ever found and the dove had to be replaced.

Liverpool Bishops

The public image of Enniskillen took a slight knock the following year, 1988, when it was reported that Liverpool Anglican Bishop, the Rt. Rev. David Sheppard, had turned down an invitation to speak at the remembrance service in St Macartin's cathedral, because the Church of Ireland minister would not extend the invitation to include the Roman Catholic Bishop of Liverpool, the Most Rev. Derek Warlock. The two men worked together on many things in Liverpool, which has a strong Irish community. One media report castigated the Enniskillen clergyman, who did not get a chance to put his point of view.

Canon McCarthy explains that the misunderstanding was that the service was in an Anglican church — it was not a town or public event. To have invited the Roman Catholic bishop would have led to sensitive problems.

After what Enniskillen had come through and the way its people had responded, there was some annoyance at the fact that the town, and the Church of Ireland community in particular, were being unfairly projected as intolerant.

Living Memorial

There is clearly dissension about a number of matters relating to Enniskillen's response and how the atrocity should be commemorated. Nevertheless, the 'spirit of Enniskillen' remains intact. And there is also a 'living memorial'.

At first, it was thought that a new youth centre for the town would be built, but this was abandoned in favour of a 'living memorial'. The Spirit of Enniskillen Bursary Scheme was launched; it is now the Spirit of Enniskillen Trust. Protestants and Catholics between the ages of 16 and 19 are involved in programmes to encourage leadership within their peer group in respecting and accepting diversity. This involves them travelling to countries where people of differing traditions have learned to respect each other. Each year at least fifty young people participate, along with ten co-ordinators. Each group of young people is mixed, having five Catholics and five Protestants, and is also mixed by gender. Over five hundred have now participated, visiting Germany, France, USA, Mexico, Latvia, Cyprus, Israel, Canada and Spain. Teenagers accepted on the scheme come from all parts of Northern Ireland, but two places are reserved each year for young people from Co. Fermanagh.

The trustees of the Enniskillen fund make a contribution of £25,000, but the then Minister of Education in Northern Ireland, Dr Brian Mawhinney initiated the scheme and was instrumental in securing European funds. A total of almost £1 million was raised, and the annual scheme is financed by the interest on this.

The scheme is a sophisticated one, drawing on the professional expertise of people involved in youthwork. On their return, the young people are engaged in debriefing and keep formal contacts. The present chairperson of the scheme is BBC broadcaster Wendy Austin, who succeeded Gerry Burns. He had served as chairperson for the first six years and points out:

> We saw this as the response of Enniskillen to the generosity of so many people throughout Northern Ireland at that time.

8: Living with Pain

Sometimes when newspapers refer to the families of those killed at Enniskillen, or those injured, there is a tendency to forget that behind every name there is an ordeal and a daily struggle. The Enniskillen families are the first to acknowledge that they are not unique by any means. Their pain is magnified thousands of times, in both communities, in towns and villages across Northern Ireland.

Political violence has wrought much heartache in Northern Ireland, especially in the past thirty years. Events in Enniskillen on 8 November 1987 brought many issues sharply into focus. However, while the challenging debate moved on, the families were left to cope with their losses. For each family that loss was different, but one thing that they all have in common is a pain that never goes away, a pain they have had to learn to live with.

Ruth Kennedy (née Johnston)

Ruth Kennedy lost her parents, Kit and Jessie Johnston:

> We were devastated at the time and we still feel so sad now. People talk about ten years. It's all right for somebody on the outside. To us it could be ten years or 110 years. To the day I die I'm going to miss them. That day it will be forgotten when we meet again. Sometimes I just look at the calendar and think, I'm a day nearer my grave.

Ruth, like her parents, is an intensely private person and found it difficult to be thrust into the public eye. She has never given interviews. Even ten years on, her grief is still palpable, and she constantly dabs tears from her eyes as she speaks of her loss:

> They were just plucked away, you kept thinking they were away on holiday. You kept thinking, they will be back. It was a long time before I could say they were killed and only recently I could say they were murdered. It really hasn't fully registered to this day that they are dead.

The trauma of 'the knock coming to the door' and being informed that her parents had been killed was overpowering, Ruth says. She still has the two dust-covered poppies that they were wearing.

The months of November and December are the worst time for her. November brings the sad time of the anniversary of the bomb, and in December there is the realisation that memories are all she has left of happy family Christmases. She dreads the time of year, and says, 'I just wish someone could take those months out of the calendar.'

Talking about her father and mother clearly helps to lift her spirits.

Margaret Veitch (née Mullan)

Margaret Veitch says that when her parents, Billy and Nessie Mullan, were killed, it was the most horrific thing imaginable: 'A part of you is taken away. I just suddenly felt like an orphan.'

Margaret was thousands of miles away when the bombing happened. An Enniskillen businesswoman, she won a UK competition for a window display in her fashion store. The prize was a two-week holiday in Kenya, on safari and in Mombasa. When she was away she thought often of her parents:

> Mummy would have just adored seeing the animals in their natural habitat.

The day before they left for home, Margaret and her husband Crawford went for a walk along a beach in Mombasa, which she recalls as 'paradise'. That night, they struck up a conversation about Northern Ireland with an English couple they had befriended:

> We sat like Tourist Board representatives, urging them to come to Northern Ireland: 'Don't worry about the Troubles, you don't see them in Fermanagh. It's so peaceful.'

The next morning, as they were leaving the hotel, Margaret picked up a newspaper. The headline flatly contradicted her words of assurance: 'Bomb in Enniskillen. 10 killed'. Worse was to come. A phone call home revealed that Mr and Mrs Mullan were among the dead.

Margaret faced a nine-hour journey back to London, and it was several more hours before she was reunited with her grieving family:

> I cried and cried and cried. You realise you're not going to touch them any more. Nobody could do anything for me. Nobody can mend a broken heart.

As time went on, she went through many emotions:

> I would wake up and my first thought would be 'Oh my God.' My stomach was sick, my heart was sore. Now I know what they mean by a sore heart. It is the most horrific feeling you can have. This goes on month after month. I just wish the politicians and people who perpetrate violence could feel it. No country is worth it — it's always the innocent people who are caught up.

Initially, her emotions were 'too raw' to talk:

> It's six months before you want anything like counselling. Then everybody else in the community has gone back to normal. It's like a wound. A scab starts to form and you think you're healing, but it takes so little to open that wound again.

There are days when she wants to talk about it, but there are also days when she simply can't:

> You just want people to not talk about it. Then after a while you think they have forgotten and you want to talk again.

Like many of the other relatives, Margaret declined interviews in the early days:

> My husband Crawford told me not to appear on television. Maybe people should have seen the way we were grieving, but unless somebody goes through it, it's hard for outsiders to see the heart.

Over the ten years, there have been many low points for Margaret: 'After a year I thought I was going off my head.' She feels angry too: 'The IRA said it was a mistake. That was one very big mistake.'

The family have a close bond. Margaret's sister, Ruth, returned home on the Sunday morning from a college reunion, only to discover the tragic news. The third sister, Joan Anderson, was sitting in her home in Long Island, New York, looking at photographs of her parents' visit that summer. She was actually holding a picture of her parents when the phone rang and she was told that they had been killed.

The Younger Family Members

Families rallied around their young people, some of whom had been injured, while others were finding it difficult to cope with the loss of a grandparent or with having witnessed the terrible event.

James Mullan was at the War Memorial but in a different area from where his parents were killed. He had nightmares about seeing the large pane of glass that came flying towards him. His son, Adam, was 10 years old and was standing in another area, with his school principal, Mr Henry Keys. James recalls the problems his son had in the early days:

> He had his tears initially, of course. He realised his grandad and grandmum were no longer with us. It was the

year he was doing his eleven plus exam and even at that age he buried himself in his work. He had heard and seen some awful things, but wasn't able to talk about it at first. Sleeping was a problem and we were told by a professional to let him come out of it himself. So we talked and talked. We went for walks together with the dog; he would have talked and told me things. Then he told his mother things and got round to telling us both together.

According to Stella Robinson, her brother, Julian Armstrong, now looks very like his father — 'he is nearly his double.' She pays tribute to Julian for the way he came through his ordeal of witnessing their parents die:

> There was a service on the first anniversary and Julian was asked to do the reading. He seemed to get the strength from nowhere.

Stella's own children too have coped with the tragedy:

> The year after it, my daughter, Nicola, got her eleven plus exam, and now my other daughter, Janice, has got engaged and Mummy and Daddy would have been so proud.

Many of the families express pride in the way the younger generations have not only coped, but used the experience to drive themselves on in their studies and chosen careers. Kathleen Armstrong is delighted that her son, Clive, recently graduated from the University of Ulster with a degree in hotel management and hospitality. He has also gained a Duke of Edinburgh gold award.

Nathan Chambers admits he often asks 'Why me?' But he quickly accepts that others were much worse than him. His left leg is half an inch shorter than his right, so he wears a built-up shoe. His fractured pelvis healed quickly and he was allowed home on Christmas Eve, although on crutches. He was determined to pass his 'O' Levels the following year at the Duke of Westminster High School, and then passed 'A' Levels at Portora Royal School before going to the University of Plymouth to qualify as a teacher. He says:

There is no point in being bitter. It is just something you have to accept and get on with life.

Ruth Kennedy has also found that her children appear determined to succeed in life as a tribute to the grand-parents they lost. Her son, Richard, 'became very wise for his age as a result of Enniskillen.' He went on to become head boy at Ballyclare High School, gained a first-class honours degree at St Andrew's University, and is now studying for a PhD at Queen's University, Belfast. He has been active in promoting better relations between the two communities in Northern Ireland. Her daughter, Sharon, has been successful in 'A' Levels and is now studying at Queen's.

James Mullan says of his son, Adam:

I think his grandparents would be very proud of him. He was head boy at Portora Royal School and went on to study medicine in Glasgow.

Just Another Atrocity

James Mullan, in common with others bereaved by the atrocity, has had to learn to live with the pain. However, he still feels anger at times:

Maybe not just as strongly as I did in the early days, but it is still there. I am still annoyed that ten years have passed and there hasn't been one single person charged with anything. If the same thing had happened across the water, I think there would have been a lot more done. We had it in writing that no stone would be unturned in the search for the perpetrators of, in their words, 'this horrific deed'. I suppose we said it was so horrendous that something will have to be done, they won't get away with it this time. I must admit I would have lived with that hope that justice would at the end be achieved.

People who are prepared to do this don't deserve to belong to society. My father always said the government should buy Rathlin Island and put them out there with enough food to provide for themselves.

But they are still doing it. I realised after a while it was just going to be another event, horrific as it was. The government weren't going to do anything special about it. There had been horrific incidents before and I thought because we were involved they would do something this time.

After a while it dawned on him that Enniskillen was going to become just another atrocity. Aileen Quinton realised this even in the days immediately after her mother, Alberta, had been killed:

I remember being annoyed by hearing people say, 'This is so awful, this must stop.' They didn't stop after the horror of people being burned in the La Mon House hotel — those victims' families must have been upset to have heard that Enniskillen was different.

Often the families are sensitive in talking about the incident, concerned that victims of other outrages will be upset by too much attention to Enniskillen. Kathleen Armstrong, who lost her husband, Ted, says:

I often go on trips with other RUC widows and one of them once said she was sick of hearing about Enniskillen. She lost her husband too. I wouldn't want to annoy good people like her.

Stella Robinson says that there are times when a 'gloom or depression' comes over her:

Sometimes I try to put it out because you keep thinking that so much has happened and so many other people have been killed. Why should mine be thought of more than anybody else's?

But it doesn't dampen the sense of injustice that the people who carried out the 1987 bombing were never caught. Bertie Megaw, whose brother, Johnny, died, says:

I find it still does annoy me that nobody was caught. A Member of Parliament told me he knew there was five people involved — that they were known. Yet they haven't been charged. It's now ten years, yet every year you see all this carry on about Bloody Sunday.

Stella Robinson, daughter of Wesley and Bertha Armstrong, believes that, 'there is somebody there who knows something and I am sure they are in Fermanagh.'

For Gladys Gault, wife of Sammy, there is anger but also a belief that the perpetrators will eventually pay:

> I do feel angry because when they killed my husband Sammy, they wrecked the whole family's life. It was never the same. You never get over it, although you learn to cope. So I do feel angry that the people who did it were never brought to justice. But one day they'll have to answer for it. If they have a conscience, it will come back at them.

Lack of Bitterness

While there certainly is a very real anger, it has not turned into any great bitterness. 'Bitterness would only destroy yourself. It would eat at you,' says Gladys Gault. She continues:

> I used to worry at the beginning that my two sons, Keith and Stephen, would become bitter. Maybe young fellas would go out and do something as a result. So I spoke to them about that, but they didn't feel bitter. They agreed with me that you couldn't hold against ordinary Catholics what one or two bad people did. The boys had their own way of dealing with it.

Stephen, who was at the Memorial with his father, has had some health problems over the ten years. He has been treated for psoriasis and has developed arthritis, although still only 28. Mrs Gault discovered some time after the tragedy that Stephen kept a scrapbook in his room about his dad. Also among the items he treasures are the poppy Sammy Gault was wearing when he was killed, along with his police cap and the union flag from his coffin. 'But he wouldn't talk much about him,' his mother says. 'Keith talks about his dad, but Stephen still clams up.'

The families' lack of bitterness, which comes through repeatedly in interviews, seems to stem in part from the fact that they all seem to focus on their memories of those who died, and not on the people who planted the bomb. Stella Robinson says:

> I just want to treasure all those memories of them. My father wouldn't have been a bitter man. I don't give much thought to those who did it because I haven't got a face, a person. I just wouldn't distort Mum and Dad's memories by thinking about somebody else anyway.

Stella's son, Stephen, was just four years old when Wesley and Bertha Armstrong were killed. Recently, when his mother referred to the fact that it is almost ten years since it happened, Stephen asked for newspaper cuttings of the time. Stella gave him scrapbooks:

> I think he just wanted to read and understand, to learn more about his grandparents.

Kathleen Armstrong was numbed by the death of her husband, Ted.

> But I never had any bitterness. Neither has my son, Clive. We just don't think about the people who did it. I think God will punish them in his own way because they have left a lot of other widows and orphans.

In talking to Ruth Kennedy too, a lack of bitterness is apparent:

> We feel no bitterness. I suppose we never stopped to consider that it was another human being that did it.

While the anger many relatives still feel is quite compatible with their lack of bitterness, it is important to acknowledge that this lack of bitterness does not necessarily stem from forgiveness.

This is one area where many would seem to differ from Gordon Wilson. However, some of the relatives interviewed make the point that what Mr Wilson actually said was not that he forgave the killers, but that he would pray for them. Many were annoyed that the media used this to portray them all as forgiving.

Gordon and Joan Wilson

While many of the bereaved simply switch off from thinking of the people who carried out the bombing, and others can think only in abstract terms, one man came face to face with those responsible for the death of his daughter.

Gordon Wilson had a secret meeting with the leadership of the IRA in 1993. It proved controversial, with criticism not only from Unionists but also from some of the other families of victims. Aileen Quinton wrote at the time in the *Sunday Life* newspaper that she was deeply saddened by his actions. She believed that it would do more harm than good and would actually encourage the IRA. Her letter, which appeared in *Sunday Life* on 11 April 1993, read:

> When my mother Alberta Quinton was murdered in the Remembrance Day bombing in 1987, I remembered my late father's advice 'never hate people, just the things they do' and I knew there were no exceptions. I was very moved and, in general, pleased with what Gordon Wilson said (at the time) as it seemed to be along the same lines and there was no mention of unconditional forgiveness.
>
> However, when I heard that the meeting between Gordon Wilson and the IRA had taken place, I felt nauseous, that somehow I had been contaminated. If his actions had, or even could have, saved just one life it would have been well worth the nausea. As it is, I believe that the situation has been made worse.
>
> The IRA were not going to stop just because they were asked to nicely. They would expect something in return and this would be the reward that they got for murdering enough people. This in turn would have sent a message to the UFF, UVF and indeed terrorist groups worldwide that if they reach their quota of murders then they will be able to influence matters. Mr Wilson was not in a position to bargain but this meeting has still given IRA a veneer of acceptability and legitimacy. This will make it easier for people to rationalise supporting them and this will be

translated into more death and suffering.

I don't think that it helps the security forces if others are talking to them. This meeting will also put pressure on those in power to follow Mr Wilson's example and then 'compromise' with evil.

I feel very strongly about each new murder and feel my pain again thinking of the families. I can well understand the emotions that lead people in desperation to cry 'We've got to do something'. However, doing nothing is surely much better than doing something that can only make things worse.

When someone you love dies in such tragic circumstances you struggle to make sense of it and you want their death to have special significance. The natural desire most of us feel to lower the level of human suffering is intensified by the idea of it being a memorial to those we love.

Working to this end can be very cathartic but whatever we have been through we have no special right to work through our pain in a way that puts the lives of others at risk. Those that are most likely to bear the brunt of the consequences of this action are the security forces, those courageous men and women who quietly risk life and limb all day and everyday in the cause of peace.

I write this letter, not because I believe that those who suffered in the past have opinions that matter more than those of others, but because like most relatively sane people my bottom line is peace, and I believe that we all have a bigger responsibility to the victims of the future than those of the past.

Joan Wilson says that she and her husband always believed, despite the criticism, that he was right to meet the IRA:

I encouraged him to go and meet them from the day the bomb went off. I just wanted to confront them face to face, to show them what they had done and ask them to stop. He always said he would be able to face his maker if he had faced them and done that.

However, the meeting exhausted him, not least because his plea for an end to the killing had little impact:

I saw him at the news conference in Belfast and he looked a tired man. That frightened me when I saw how exhausted he was and how deflated and defeated he was. The whole family was drained. My son, Peter, was in a dreadful state in case he wouldn't get back safely, although we were promised nothing would happen.

I was in Gortatole with the junior orchestra who were giving a wee concert. I was trying to pretend that everything was normal. I came home at 8.30 and Peter was pacing the floor and Julie Anne was just desperate. About 9.30 the phone rang to say he was back in Donegal safely — that the whole thing was over and he would be home in forty minutes.

He came in and he was just pale and exhausted. He said they were not going to give up, they didn't seem to care how long they went on or how many people were killed. He saw how serious they were. He off-loaded for hours.

Some people said he gave them credibility. We couldn't see that in any shape or form. I just wanted myself or him to look into the eyes of the people who had been behind that and say, 'Don't do it. It is achieving nothing and one day you will be judged for it. Murder is wrong.'

According to his wife, Gordon Wilson accepted the criticism:

He didn't mind. Everybody was entitled to their point of view. He was always aware that we spoke only for ourselves. But I think he had to talk about things. If he had bottled it up, it would have killed him. So he talked and it killed him.

Social worker David Bolton also believes that he was right to meet the IRA:

It was an amazing, courageous thing to do. To go through the dark alone, to be met and handed from one to another, it took guts. I know others feel that he was wrong to do it, but I feel it was right. The important point is it was part of his own journey and everyone who has suffered out of Enniskillen has had to travel their own journey.

We can be critical of each other, but at least allow us all our own journey.

The difficulty in coping is ongoing. In 1996, at a time when Gladys Gault appeared to be doing well, a large bomb exploded outside the Killyhevlin Hotel in Enniskillen. She heard the loud explosion and knew that her son, Stephen, was at the golf club that night. 'You think you have recovered but I just went to pieces that night,' she recalls.

The Bomb Site

The Enniskillen families have had some dark moments in private over the past ten years, but they have shown remarkable fortitude in overcoming them. There is clearly some residual anger, particularly over the fact that nobody has been brought to justice. Another thing that upsets many of them is the fact that nothing has been done with the bomb site itself. The building was flattened but there was a lot of rubble still there until recently, surrounded by wooden hoardings, which became scruffy themselves through time. A plaque has been placed on the actual War Memorial twenty yards away, but the place where the people died under the rubble is still in a poor state.

The bomb site is at the top of Belmore Street, in a prominent place at the east end of Enniskillen, where much of the traffic from the main routes from Belfast and the east of Northern Ireland comes into town. It is a central location and most people going about their business pass it every day. It is a constant physical scar on the landscape.

Some of the relatives were reluctant to go near the place where their relatives were killed. Margaret Veitch's shop is in Belmore Street, a few hundred yards from the bomb site. For the first year she found herself unable to walk on that side of the street.

For Aileen Quinton, however, it was important to see it. Two days after her mother's death, she travelled the few miles with her brothers to stand at the site:

Gordon Wilson became a famous figure, a good 'story' in media terms. In 1993, he accepted the invitation of the then Taoiseach, Albert Reynolds, to sit in the Irish Senate. He was invited to speak all over the world, received numerous peace awards and met leading world figures. However, according to Joan Wilson, all of this took its toll:

> There is no doubt that all the pressure and publicity was severe on him. Julie Anne did not like the publicity, she hated it. She thought for the sake of her father he should have had more privacy. Peter did not like it either. Definitely not.
>
> Very often, Gordon would guide people away — he didn't want it to be the Wilsons all the time.

She remembers her own moments of private tears:

> After the bomb, December 1987 passed and every day there was something. I just didn't have time to grieve until January really. Then it hit hard. I remember going out to Castle Coole to take a long walk. I remember seeing the first snowdrop and a flood of tears just came. I cried uncontrollably and then I turned to come back past the snowdrops. I sobbed and sobbed and then suddenly it stopped. I felt a cleansing and a healing and I thought, well it is all right to cry. Peter and Julie Anne missed their sister too, don't forget.

Just before Christmas 1994, seven years after Marie's death in the bombing, the Wilson's only son, Peter, was killed in a car crash. Gordon Wilson died of a heart attack at home the following year. Mrs Wilson says:

> Ten years back, we were a complete family. I had this great fear that I would forget Marie's voice, but today I thought, 'I can hear her.' The three of them are always there.

Aileen Quinton

For Aileen Quinton, the early part of the journey of the past ten years was tough. Having heard of her mother's death, she immediately returned from London where she works:

By the time I got home, the house was pretty full. The kitchen was taken over by family and friends who were manning the teapot and a lot of people were calling. The thing was totally dream-like. At the back of my mind I thought, I must go and get my mother, she will want to see them all.

Aileen has since said that the shock in the early stages had a numbing effect. After a few weeks she returned to London and went back to work:

> I went through all the emotions and I hadn't a clue what I was doing. I carried on until February and then I couldn't cope any more so I simply ran away. I didn't even tell them I was going — I came back to Enniskillen and my brothers hid me. I did think about suicide. I didn't necessarily think I wanted to die; I just didn't want to be conscious.
>
> There were days I stayed up in my room. I couldn't even face a normal conversation

Aileen was off work for almost two years. She has learned a lot from her experience during those times. She has written leaflets about trauma, and produced a video on the subject. On one occasion she was invited to take part in a group therapy session by the Royal Navy who were using her video as part of their trauma therapy programme.

She has also written an article for *Welfare World* in which she discusses the problems faced by the friends and relatives of disaster victims. In the article, 'After the Disaster', she points out that the country at large often expects the people involved to be inspirational with their courage:

> Disaster victims feel under great pressure to be brave. . . . In many cases what is taken to be bravery is merely shock preventing any show of emotion. If victims are praised for this, it can make it very difficult for them later to show what they are really feeling when some of the shock wears off.[1]

She is concerned that at such times 'community leaders' take control of events:

What can happen is that control is assumed b[...] munity leaders, e.g. clergy and priests, councill[...] services and fund trustees. They do not realise [...] tance of giving this control to the people who [...] most adversely affected.

Moral Support

Aileen Quinton's knowledge of post-traumatic [...] helps people in other places to deal with their [...] Other Enniskillen families have also shown a gre[...] osity of spirit in helping others. Joan Wilson has [...] relatives of other victims of the Troubles, inclu[...] parents of Catholic taxi driver, Michael McGold[...] was murdered by Loyalists in Lurgan in 1996, [...] mother of British soldier, Trooper Stephen Restor[...] was shot dead at an army checkpoint in Februa[...] These families who have suffered through violer[...] in constant touch, giving each other moral suppo[...]

Some of the families who lost loved ones in the [...] killen bomb have supported each other too. Ha[...] ceived invitations to private functions to meet [...] such as the Queen Mother, they would use these [...] tunities to discuss their common experiences. S[...] the women would then get together informally fo[...] or coffee, to chat about their difficulties. The me[...] found it more difficult to open up and would mai[...] 'stiff upper lip'.

The families have received support from une[...] quarters too. A woman in Cambridge in England co[...] Julian Armstrong having seen press coverage [...] bombing. His sister, Stella, explains:

> She is Jenny Gaudon and is a friend of John and [...] Major. She has painted their portraits and is going [...] paint Nelson Mandela's portrait in South Africa. [...] such a lovely person. She said she was reading the [...] and my father just 'jumped out of the page'. Sh[...] poppies for me and would tell me the history of the [...] She rings me up every Remembrance Sunday.

It was about trying to see reality. I hadn't seen the body, so I could indulge myself that maybe it had been a big mistake. I wanted to see the site. A policeman stopped us on the way and asked us where we were going, as two of the funerals were taking place. My brother, Christopher, just took a deep breath and said, 'We are just going in to find out where my mother was murdered on Sunday.' There was no point in saying anything different.

I remember seeing people lined up at the site. I just looked at it, a place where I had stood loads of times. There was the phone box where I used to ring up my father if I was in town and wanted a lift home. I just looked at it and thought, 'Where is she?'

James Mullan drives past the site half a dozen times a day:

I didn't at the start. I would have driven anywhere — gone round the town any other way rather than drive past it. I finally managed to do it. To go there on later Remembrance Days was traumatic. But I still do and I think of my parents every day.

I honestly think something should have been done as regards the site. The Government should have done whatever was necessary to purchase it.

Kathleen Armstrong has to pass the site every day too. But she says:

I think that corner is just terrible. If I have to walk past it, I just shudder. It brings it all back.

Gladys Gault also finds it difficult to look at the place where her husband died:

Looking at that hoarding still there annoys me. For a long time, I wouldn't even walk on that side of the street. I avoided it without even realising. We went back as a family to lay a wreath and stood with some of the other families. But that thing is still there. It is a constant reminder.

Stella Robinson says that passing the site used to bother her more. However, her main feelings are of sadness for her parents. She says of the site:

I just don't look at it. When I'm on my own, I grieve and think about my mother and father. That alone gets me low enough without getting angry when I look at the site as well.

The difficulties in creating a garden of remembrance on the site have been dealt with in Chapter 7. Having decided that this idea would not be feasible, the problem still remained of exactly what should be done with it. Monsignor Seán Cahill explains:

It was very sensitive and we didn't want to put something there that would stir up emotions. There was never any intention on our behalf to be insensitive. It was very difficult in the light of the enormity of the tragedy to know what to do. Therefore, you might say it was a kind of paralysis — we waited and waited.

The best hope for something positive came in 1995 when a plan was unveiled to build a splendid six-storey centre on the site. At a cost of £6 million it was anticipated that not only would it transform the look of the area, but it would also provide educational and economic facilities for the benefit of both sides of the community. The Catholic Church agreed to release the site.

The 'University Partnership', a body specially formed to see the project through, put it forward for funding from the Millennium Commission in Britain, which is financing a number of projects. However, imaginative as the plan was, it was not included in the funding list, much to the disappointment of those who formulated it and, indeed, the community in general in Enniskillen.

The project team is pressing ahead with plans to attract other funding. But for the moment, the bomb site remains a blot on the landscape — a sad reminder to the families and an eyesore for the many tourists who come to admire Enniskillen's beautiful lakes and to visit the famous War Memorial.

In September 1997, a digger moved in to begin clearing the rubble. In the absence of any project to develop the site properly, the authorities decided to spend £15,000 in tidying it up. The idea was to grass over the ground and erect a more attractive display board to make things look more respectable in the short term, particularly in time for the tenth anniversary of the bombing.

Ronnie Hill

Aside from the mental anguish endured by many whose relatives were killed, the bombing has also left many suffering physically. A number of people who were dug out from under the rubble survived. But, to a greater or lesser extent, they have had to endure physical pain. Several people have had to cope with injuries that have changed their lives.

The best-known of the injured is Ronnie Hill. The former headmaster of Enniskillen High School, he took a Bible class for teenagers at Enniskillen Presbyterian church on the morning of the bomb. Having let the class out early, he had joined them at the War Memorial when the bomb went off. Mr Hill, who had recovered from heart by-pass surgery two years earlier, was buried under rubble, and rescuers spotted a gloved hand sticking out. He was initially taken to the Erne hospital, and then rushed by helicopter to Altnagelvin hospital in Derry. He had fractures to his skull, jaw, shoulder and pelvis. He received thirty-seven stitches in his face and, after surgery, was brought to intensive care.

Two days after the bomb, he went into a coma, from which he has never emerged. He spent five weeks in the Derry hospital, some of it on a life-support machine. His wife, Noreen Hill, recalls:

> The nurses were forever telling us he was dying, he wouldn't see morning. Quite often, rumours were going round Enniskillen that he was dead. Maybe it was after the Thursday night, Thursday was always his really bad night. I was told afterwards that everyone who was seriously injured at Enniskillen had their bad night on a Thursday. There was no reason for that.

After five weeks in which Mrs Hill sat by her husband's bedside every day, Ronnie Hill was transferred back to the Erne hospital in Enniskillen. He remained there for five years, still in a coma. Mrs Hill travelled from her home in the town every day to sit with her husband, reading the Bible to him and talking to him. Then she bought a large house in Holywood, Co. Down, and opened a residential home. This allowed her to provide a special room with round-the-clock care for her husband.

Liquid food is pumped into his system and an artificial trachea is inserted to remove a build-up of mucus in his windpipe. His wife explains:

> I sit with him in the evenings. When the mucus gathers, he needs suction, so I do that for him. Or if he needed water or feed in the pump I would change that for him. The night staff come in and give him a bed bath: he can't move so he has to be turned. When I'm sitting, if he makes a noise, I would speak over to him. I sometimes pray with him, maybe do Bible readings. When I started doing his readings he would start swallowing and yawning. He was listening and that's how we know that he does hear and he does understand.

In addition to swallowing and yawning, occasionally Ronnie Hill's eyelids blink. Mrs Hill says: 'The doctors aren't convinced, but we are convinced that he understands.'

Ronnie Hill was born in Dublin in 1931 and educated at St Andrew's College there. He moved to Northern Ireland in the early 1950s to take up a teaching post at Mourne Grange School near Kilkeel, Mrs Hill's home town. The couple married in 1956 and went to Africa for six years where Mr Hill was a missionary teacher. In the 1960s, they returned when Ronnie took up a teaching post in Omagh, and the couple then moved briefly to Rathfriland and on to Kesh in Co. Fermanagh in 1969. Five years later, in 1974, Mr Hill began his long and happy association with Enniskillen High School. Mrs Hill recalls the couple's busy and rewarding life:

His work with the school was very important to him. I said it was work first and family second; over in the school they said it was family first and work second. We had a very good life in Enniskillen. We enjoyed life. Ronnie and I played bridge in the golf club; he played golf and was on quite a few committees. He was in the Rotary Club for a while but he found it was taking up too much of his time. He was in the school from 8.30 in the morning until 6.30 in the evening. I think his life was the children. His one aim was to make sure anyone in his care got a good education. No matter how poor they were, he always said there was something they would be good at.

The change in lifestyle following the bomb is stark. But Mrs Hill, daughters Avril, Marilyn and Siobhan, and son Keith are determined not to let it get them down. Ronnie is still a major part of the family life. Keith has two children, 9-year-old Stephanie, and 3-year-old Christine. Siobhan's son, Christopher, is a year old. Mrs Hill says:

Of course he has missed his grandchildren, he would have loved them. Grandpa has never been any other way than in bed. Sometimes the wee ones come out with things about him and you think it is so sad.

The adults leave bars of chocolate or sweets under Mr Hill's pillow so that when the children visit, they get a gift from him before they go home.

Once, when Christine was younger, she asked permission from her father to do something. He refused, so she went in and asked her grandad if she could do it. The adults enjoyed the moment listening to her on the sound monitor that lies beside Mr Hill all the time!

However, there have been times when Mrs Hill has found it difficult to cope:

Many a time I was down, but the Lord was always there to lift me up. You can't live in the past, you have to take each day at a time. I think that should apply to everyone because nobody knows what is going to happen. . . . I don't dwell on it. I don't think, 'Oh poor me, look what I have come through'.

George Evans

Another man injured in the bomb has shown fierce determination and courage in getting back to almost a normal family life again. Policeman George Evans was 29 when the bomb exploded behind him. The video footage shows him minutes afterwards, in great distress as he is pulled from the rubble. However, when he got to hospital doctors initially thought that he was not too seriously injured. They soon discovered, though, that a blow to the head had caused damage to his brain. A hole was bored in his skull to relieve the pressure, but when this failed he was taken by helicopter to the Royal Victoria Hospital in Belfast. Surgeons decided to operate immediately, taking part of his skull away and removing a tiny bit of his brain. The pressure eased.

When he awoke in hospital, a woman was sitting beside him but he did not recognise her. She had to tell him, 'I'm your wife, Veronica.'

George Evans faced over three years of rehabilitation. Not only could he not remember his wife or his two little daughters, but he had no recollection of the bombing. Doctors gave him little chance of walking again.

Christmas 1987 was a difficult time for the Evans family. George was allowed home briefly to be with Veronica, and their children, 4-year-old Karen, and Joanne, who was just over a year. Veronica was pregnant with their third child.

In an article in a police magazine,[2] George recalls that he would look at his little girl across the room and ask his wife who she was. She would explain that it was Karen, his daughter. George explains: 'The name would stick in your head for two seconds and then you'd forget again.'

The following May, their third daughter, Lisa, was born. In those early days, George himself needed constant care. He had to eat liquidised food, was very weak and could only stay up for ten minutes at a time. He pays tribute to his wife:

When I look back there were times she could have left. There was a lot of pressure on her looking after the children on her own, because I was actually a baby then too.[2]

The long road back to recovery began in earnest in a rehabilitation centre in England. Initially he was bitter and angry, but experts advised him to rid himself of the bitterness and channel his emotion into getting well.

George had to have a steel plate inserted in his head to replace the piece of skull that was removed. Then he had to learn to walk and talk again. There were many frustrations. Often he would know what he wanted to say, but couldn't get the words out. Regaining his memory was a difficult process, but he was encouraged to remember events from years ago. He learned to write again and would write one-line letters to Veronica. Despite the many setbacks, he defied the odds and walked again.

After nearly four years, George returned to work on light duties. Recently, the family moved to a beautiful new home, and they are looking to the future with confidence. They are remarkable examples of what a fighting spirit can overcome.

Jim Dixon

The man with probably the most severe physical injuries was Jim Dixon. He was just 50 when the Reading Rooms wall collapsed onto him:

I was struck on the head, on the side of the face which did a lot of damage, and the building fell on my body and smashed my pelvis, hips and legs. The surgery went on for about nine hours. I have steel plates in my head. My eye sockets were blown out. They couldn't find some of the bones in my head because they had disintegrated.

He points to the side of his head:

The whole face was smashed in here — that is all skin grafted around my two eyes. I had brain damage, spine damage; my tongue was paralysed; I had a jaw bone missing; I couldn't open my mouth. They patched me up, took bits of bone out and built up the roof of my mouth.

Mr Dixon cannot close his eyes. He has no tear ducts and keeps a tube of ointment with him at all times, which he must use constantly to keep his eyes moist. 'I live in severe pain,' he says. 'The nerves at the back of my eyes were terribly badly damaged.'

Surgeons told Mr Dixon that he needed a greater power than theirs — 'it was God that saved me.' He couldn't walk when he came out of hospital:

I couldn't even stand. My balance was completely gone. The biggest job was to feed me because I couldn't open my mouth. I couldn't suck because the swallow at the back of my throat was damaged, still is. I had trouble swallowing, it gets into my windpipe. We are wonderfully made, you know.

Ten years on, Jim Dixon is in constant pain:

But I try not to take tablets in case they upset my stomach and give me depression and all sorts of things. They wanted to put me on morphine, but I wouldn't go on it.

The physical effects of the bomb are plain to see, and Mr Dixon has been told that he could face further operations to his jaw. Occasionally during our conversation, he gets up and walks around the room. His wife, Anna, explains that he deals with pain by keeping very active:

The more pain Jim is in, the more he has to get out. A normal person would want to sit in the chair or go to bed. Jim will go out and cut a hedge or do some hard work, cut the grass or something, to get over the pain. When he gets home, he feels he must be doing something, then his mind will switch off. Then he thinks he should be at something else, so he has a hundred jobs on at the one time.

Thankfully, Jim has always been a goer or he wouldn't have been able to rise above his problems. He has always had great determination.

The couple have friends in several areas in South Africa,

and a recent holiday involved ten flights in a few weeks across the country. Anna Dixon explains:

> Our way of life has been disrupted. My priorities are changed. Anything to help Jim. He is suffering, so it is the least I can do. I don't always feel like it but I will go.

The couple are also supported by their grown-up daughters, Suzanne, Sharon and Serena.

'We can cope with all the worries in life because of God's help,' says Mr Dixon. He is a talented musician and finds music a great therapy. In his den upstairs he plays the electric accordion. He has an old theatre organ and an organ out in his garage. He says:

> I do a lot of charity music and play at gospel missions. I couldn't play for a while after the bomb because of the brain damage. My hands wouldn't work for me, but it came back. Not as good as it used to be. I get up and play at different socials and things. When I am up on the platform my head would be spinning. I would be confused, terrified. I can't even hear what I am playing because the sound is all muffled. When I am up there, I do think to myself, 'What on earth has me up here?' I think they must be very gracious people to listen to me.

---

1 Quinton, A. (1996): 'After the Disaster' in *Welfare World* (The Journal of the Association of Welfare Workers in England), September: 5–9.
2 Evans, G. (1991): Article in *Police Beat*, December: 20–21.

9: Keeping the Faith

Clearly, the people most directly affected by the Enniskillen bomb have suffered much, and have had to cope with burdens and experiences that have changed their lives forever. To be subjected to such suffering might have made people question their faith in God, even abandon it. However, in a number of cases in Enniskillen, the opposite happened, and people looking for help found it in a renewal or enrichment of their Christian faith.

What came across in talking to many of the victims and the bereaved was a strong sense of deep religious experience.

Stephen Ross

Stephen Ross is now 25 and lives near Basingstoke in the south of England where he works for an insurance company. Ironically, having been so close to death himself ten years ago, he now deals with death claims on a daily basis.

Stephen is a member of the Independent Evangelical Church, which has similar beliefs to the Baptist Church. Around the area there are posters with the dramatic photograph of Stephen taken in the days after the bomb at Enniskillen — surgery to repair agonising facial injuries is held in place by a steel cage bolted into his jaw and forehead. Above the photo, the poster's message reads: 'Back from the brink of death to life. Bomb victim tells his story here tonight.'

Stephen has a remarkable story to tell and he has been telling it regularly to audiences comprising as few as twenty people and as many as a thousand. He believes that God brought him here and he must use his experience to bring the Christian message to people.

In stark contrast to the gruesome injuries of 1987, there is now no visual evidence of that day — his blond, handsome looks are intact. It is quite a recovery, considering that a huge slab of masonry landed on his face. Two teams of surgeons at the Altnagelvin Hospital in Derry spent five and a half hours operating on him. One team worked on his left leg, which they feared they might have to amputate below the knee. The other team operated on facial injuries: his nose was broken, the roof of his mouth was split from front to back, his five front teeth were gone, he had fractures to the bones underneath his eyes and in his forehead, and his jaw was badly broken. Stephen's father, Graham, was waiting anxiously outside the operating theatre, and at one stage a surgeon came out to tell him that his son was very weak and might not survive the surgery. Stephen is full of admiration for the doctors:

> They virtually rebuilt my face from the inside out. I don't really know how they did it, but it involved pushing the bones back into place. They used a steel cage to hold the bones in my face. The cage was held in place by boring holes in the bits of jaw bone that were stable, and they also wired my teeth together.

The teenager was in intensive care for six days and in hospital for five weeks, his leg in plaster up to his waist. During that time he could take in only fluids, and his weight dropped by four stone. He says:

> I can still feel the breaks under my eyes and the sockets. I have a wire permanently fixed in my palate; the shape of my mouth has changed a lot. If I yawn too wide or eat really hard food, sometimes my jaw would start crunching or cracking. One of my legs is slightly longer than the other, but I can walk and run normally. I just have to be a bit careful playing football.

Stephen's recuperation was long and painful. He was off school for over five months in a crucial year in which he was due to sit 'O' Levels. But he was given two hours' private tuition a day, and his father, a teacher, helped him as well. The following summer, seven months after the bomb, he sat and passed five subjects and passed three more the following November. His indomitable spirit saw him recognised with a United Kingdom 'Champion Children of the Year' award, which he received from Princess Diana at a presentation in London.

He and his friend, Nathan Chambers, who was also injured in the bomb, joined in a project in 1989 with a number of other children affected. Along with the singer, Dana, they produced a song, written by Patrick Grant, brother of singer Eddie Grant. It was about community spirit. Stephen was also given a place on the Canadian 'Marie Wilson Voyage of Hope' scheme (see Chapter 11).

Stephen became something of a media personality in those hectic days, but it was in the quietness of his own home that he would reflect on the fact that at the tender age of 15 he had already come so close to death. He received over 800 letters and what he describes as 'a huge box of cards' from Ireland, England, the United States and Canada. Many of them were from Christian friends, saying that they were praying for him. It made him think more about God:

> I remember becoming a Christian when I was 13, after hearing a man speak about his son and four others being killed in a car crash. It challenged me to think, you never know when life or death situations are going to strike. But after a while I wasn't really living out my faith. After the bomb, a Methodist minister came to see me and gave me a Bible with Rom. 8: 28 marked on it: 'In all things God works for the good of those who love him and are called according to His purpose.' That verse stuck with me and I began to realise that God had a purpose through the whole experience that I had. I began to read the Bible more and realised how relevant it was. The Bible wasn't just something that was written 2,000 years

ago, but something that was relevant to me now.

> One of the things I realised was how weak my body was, how weak human beings are, but where your real strength lies. It made me realise how unpredictable life is.

With a smile, he adds:

> It also makes you thankful for your food. When you go thirty days without food, you become thankful for what you get.

He recalls the first anniversary of the bomb, when the six members of his family, including his father and mother, returned to the Remembrance Sunday ceremony:

> It was quite upsetting. We were standing quite far away from where I was the day the bomb went off. But it was traumatic for my family and me. I just felt empty and downcast, thinking about the suffering I had been through and the people who had been lost.

He says that his 'real Christianity experience' has deepened, and now he spends much of his life sharing that with others. It also helped him to deal with his natural feelings of anger after the bombing:

> I did feel angry, but as a Christian I turn that over to God and ask God to take that anger from me. I am also able to ask God to forgive the people who did it, if it is His will. As a Christian myself, I believe I will be accountable if I break God's law. In that sense I am no different to the people who did this. I have prayed for those people. I can forgive them. I know some people don't hold that view and therefore I don't want to offend or hurt people who have lost loved ones as a result of the explosion. I can only speak for myself, but I can identify with what Gordon Wilson said.

Stephen admits that he does feel anger coming at times when he hears people from Sinn Féin 'actively supporting violence'. He says:

> To me terrorists aren't open to reason, they aren't logical. But the people who support them are logical. Therefore, to me they are as accountable as the people who pull the

trigger or plant the bomb. But when I get those feelings of anger, I have to turn it off. It is not going to do me any good and I turn it over to God. I am not opposed to talking to these people. It was significant what they said to Gordon Wilson. Obviously they showed little remorse for killing his daughter and made it clear they wouldn't give up their struggle. But I have no objections to talking to them even if they don't give up arms. Every avenue should be explored.

Stephen is committed now to living a Christian life:

What I believe as a Christian has had a real, long and lasting impact on my life from the time of the bomb until now. It would have been easy for me to become bitter. I think if you did, it would affect you emotionally, you could become a warped person. I wasn't going to let these people or anybody else ruin my life, so I was determined to get on with it.

The year after the bomb, he transferred from Enniskillen High School to Portora Royal School where he passed 'A' Levels. He then spent four years doing Business Studies at the University of Ulster, Jordanstown. Having first gained a post as a trainee manager with C&A in England, he then got a job with an insurance company. He says:

As a Christian, my faith is a large part of my life. I have learned to take each day as it comes. I've learned not to depend on my own strength. God has been with me and I have had so many good experiences; I began to see how I should live as a Christian.

Julian Armstrong

Another young man who was caught up in the explosion as a teenager also holds firmly rooted Christian beliefs. Julian Armstrong had to get over the trauma of watching his mother and father, Wesley and Bertha, die on either side of him. He was just 16 then and almost didn't go to the War Memorial on the fateful morning. The night before, his mother overcame his reluctance and per-suaded him to go to keep his father happy. Julian's memory of the moments when the bomb exploded are still vivid:

> I just remember in that two minutes praying to God and saying, 'If you are out there, God, help me in this.' I was able to sleep peacefully that night, I believe God was looking after me.

Julian's physical injuries were slight:

> I had a cut on my head and a neck brace on as well. I had a few cuts and bruises on my legs, that's all. The only thing left is a little scar that hurts a bit when the sun comes out.

In the weeks and months after the bomb, he had differing emotions:

> I felt confused for a time. I came out virtually unhurt, others were killed. There are people like Mr Hill who went into a coma. It scares you being in between two people who died. I was nearly at death's door, and being that close to death makes you think of life in a totally different perspective.

Julian had had a normal childhood, but his life changed dramatically after that day:

> Sometimes I think, was there a sign before to show us what would happen? I had a nightmare where a robber came in and killed both my parents. After the bomb happened, there was this total change. I was 16 years old and had to grow up very quickly.

He lived with his older brother, Trevor. Their sisters helped by returning regularly to cook and clean the house. Practical things were taken care of, but it was Julian's ability to deal with the trauma that concerned his family:

> I was finding counsellors a bit false; it was easier talking to friends and family. There were things like the gory details that I wouldn't talk about. One night at the start, the nurse had to call my sister in the middle of the night because I was shouting. I don't remember that. I remember thinking once, 'I have got to eat this meal even though I

don't want it. Mum would like me to eat it, she wouldn't want me to suffer too.'

A local Christian family, the Pierces, helped Julian considerably:

They just went that extra mile, made friends with me. They showed me Christianity in a different light, that it wasn't boring.

Although his parents, who attended the Methodist church, were both Christians, Julian says that prior to the bomb, he found church boring,

But after the bomb I started thinking about things. I think when you suffer like that you search for things more. Suffering brings you close to God.

The year after the bomb, Julian left Fermanagh College to go to Cardiff University where he studied banking and finance. After three years, he applied to do a year at Cliff Bible College in Sheffield. One night he attended a meeting, where a service at Earl's Court, London, was being relayed by live video link. The preacher was American evangelist Dr Billy Graham. Julian recalls:

It was as if he was speaking to me. I remember thinking, 'I want to become a Christian, I need to do this.' I got up publicly and went to the front. People do it differently, but I felt I should do that; Paul Pierce went up at that time too. I remember thinking, 'There is hope, there is a future. God can provide that hope and future for me because He suffered and died for me and He understands what suffering is. His only son died on the Cross for everybody.'

This 'born-again' experience brought him peace of mind:

I felt more security to my life because until then I was unsure. I believe God has healed my life and helped me to cope with those memories. It was traumatic to see my parents like that, but I have just got to look at my parents as they were before the bomb happened.

His faith helped him to deal with difficult emotions:

A few weeks after the bomb I suppose I was bitter against Catholics. I grew up in a Protestant estate, so in Northern Ireland there is this kind of prejudice anyway. It took me some time afterwards to think about the whole issue. I shouldn't have that bitterness against Catholics — there are bad eggs on both sides. I don't feel any hatred towards the people who did it. I suppose if I met them now, I would ask them why they did it. As a Christian I try my best to live up to being a Christian; it is hard and sometimes you feel down, but Jesus says, pray for them.

I wasn't going to go out and shoot them, but I believe in justice for those who murder people. They call themselves prisoners of war, but they have murdered innocent people. There is a lot of healing to be done in this land after twenty-five years of hurt and violence.

Having completed his year at Bible College, Julian returned to Enniskillen, but after six months at home he left to take up a post in Newcastle, Co. Down, with 'Friends in the West', a Christian organisation, which helps to relieve suffering in Africa. Julian's role is to look after the administrative needs of a choir of African children, aged between five and twelve, who tour Ireland giving concerts to raise funds for projects back home.

Julian lives in Kilkeel, in a scenic area at the foot of the Mourne Mountains. He says: 'I know I won't forget what happened. But I am content now.'

Noreen Hill

Noreen Hill has also found succour in her religion. She tends her husband, Ronnie, who is still in a coma.

The year 1987 had been extremely difficult for Noreen Hill even before the November bomb. She was diagnosed as having cancer and had an operation in February. Then she had a course of radiotherapy, followed by a course of chemotherapy. On Remembrance Sunday she felt too weak to take her usual place beside her husband at the ceremony. They had always met up after Mr Hill's Bible class.

Noreen Hill was sitting at home when the bomb went off. She recalls:

> I looked at the clock. It was seventeen minutes to eleven. That's the thing I always remember. I heard it and I started to cry. My daughter, Siobhan, came downstairs and I said there was a bomb at the cenotaph. Where else would it be? Or else it was a sixth sense. I knew Ronnie was injured.

As it turned out, Ronnie Hill was one of the most seriously hurt and he has never regained consciousness. Still physically weak from her treatment to defeat cancer, Noreen Hill had to summon incredible reserves of strength for the next ten years. While he was in the Erne hospital in Enniskillen, she spent several hours with him every day. He continues to need constant nursing at the residential home she bought in Holywood, Co. Down, where nursing staff and carers are employed to look after up to twenty residents. The Hills' daughter, Marilyn, returned from the United States to run the home, which was bought so that the family could provide the facilities that Ronnie needed. It is a remarkable story of devotion.

As well as spending time with her husband, Noreen Hill gets to know the other elderly residents. In the early days of setting up the home, she had to spend long hours looking after Ronnie and getting through the other work. On occasions, she worked through two days and a night; once she didn't get to bed for eighty-four hours. But she refuses to feel sorry for herself:

> Once you do that you are lost. There are thousands of people out there who have come through far more than I have ever come through. People say, 'Look what she has come through, she is so strong.' I am not strong, I am just as you see, as weak as the next person. But I have a very strong God and he is there to help me. He is there for everyone, but some people don't rely on him as much. I had no option because I was weak after the chemotherapy.

Noreen Hill says that in the early days after the bomb,

the family was in shock and could just take one day at a time. When she suffered memory lapses, such as forgetting telephone numbers, she realised that part of her mind had closed down. In those early days, she also realised that her God prevented her from becoming bitter:

> The Lord could never have allowed me to be bitter because I couldn't have carried that burden. The same with Gordon Wilson. If he had to carry that burden of bitterness, he would have been dead long before he did die. God gave him the words. At the hospital when I went to find Ronnie, the first person I remember meeting was Monsignor Cahill. But I didn't see a Catholic priest, I saw a friend. From the very first minutes I didn't feel bitter.

She is firm in her belief that God intervened in this and in other ways:

> I always said that Satan caused the bomb, but the Lord chose the people. All those who died that day were Christians. They were all prepared to die. If the Lord had taken the biggest rogue in Enniskillen, he wasn't prepared to die. So, hopefully he was left so that he could repent of his sins. Maybe they would realise that one minute you are well, the next minute you are no more. It can happen any time, whether out in the car, a heart attack or if you are murdered.

Mrs Hill spreads this message when she addresses church meetings, Methodist women's groups and Presbyterian women's groups. She has also been interviewed extensively by journalists from newspapers and the broadcast media, attracted by her display of faith. As a result of such media coverage, she often has complete strangers coming up to her to wish her well. She says simply, 'I wouldn't be here today without my faith.'

Sustained by her beliefs, Noreen Hill also refuses to give up hope that one day Ronnie will be better. She takes inspiration from the fact that a young man, in a coma following the Hillsborough football disaster in England, recently started showing signs of understanding:

A year ago we would have said that would never happen. Somebody has pointed out to me that maybe part of your brain has gone, but there is so much of the brain that you don't ever use and that can take over. There is no guarantee that it won't happen for Ronnie, there is no guarantee it will. That is in the Lord's hands and we have got to accept that. There is a purpose in everything he allows to happen. You accept that we might not know the purpose on earth, but when we meet we will know.

Before I left Mrs Hill, she brought me down to see Ronnie. 'It's Denzil McDaniel to see you, Ronnie,' she told him. But there was no recognition, such as flickering of the eyelids or swallowing. I remarked that he looked exactly the same as he had when I had last visited him, over five years ago, in the Erne Hospital. 'He has no stresses or strains,' explains Noreen Hill, who clearly relies on her God to help her to shoulder all her own stresses and strains.

Kathleen Armstrong

Another woman who has shared her burden with the Lord is Kathleen Armstrong, who lost her husband, Ted, in the bombing. On the day of the bomb, Kathleen had changed her routine of standing with her husband at the ceremony. On Sunday mornings, women in the Presbyterian church take turns at making coffee for the congregation. She had switched her turn from the previous week and was walking across to the church hall with a bag of biscuits, which Ted had bought. On the way, she saw Ted at his usual place at the Reading Rooms wall, and waved over to him. Seconds later, the bomb exploded.

Ted Armstrong was killed, but apart from a cut on the hand, his wife seemed to be physically unhurt. However, she had severe diarrhoea and vomiting throughout the day. She explains:

It was only the next day when I was dressing when I noticed my stomach covered in black bruising right round to the middle of my back. I was bleeding through the kidney for three or four weeks. A plank or something had hit me without me realising.

Doctors are unsure whether this injury was a contributory factor to some devastating news which Kathleen Armstrong received some years later:

> In 1994 I got the shock of being told I had a cancerous tumour. I had ovarian cancer. I had six months of chemotherapy in Belvoir Park hospital in Belfast and four weeks of radium treatment. The doctors and nurses gave me tender loving care and I went through the treatment smiling and thanking God for giving me strength.

In the past ten years, in addition to her husband's death and her own battle against cancer, Kathleen Armstrong lost her mother, who died from Alzheimer's Disease in 1991, and her father, who died in 1997:

> I often ask 'Why me?' but we cannot blame God. Every day I say, 'The Lord is our Shepherd and He'll lead the way.'

She is particularly thankful for the special bond she has with her son, Clive, who was only 16 when his father was killed.

> It is hard bringing up a boy on your own, but he has been so good to me. We supported each other. Clive would go out to his father's grave, but he would never go with me. He would say he had been out to Daddy's grave today.

After Mrs Armstrong became ill, Clive transferred back from college in Scotland to finish his studies at the University of Ulster, so that he could be nearer to his mother.

When she was told of her illness, Kathleen Armstrong was visited by the Rev. David Cupples, who, she remembers, said 'a lovely prayer'. Then she was visited by a family friend, Ken Stephenson, who also prayed with her. She recalls:

> After the two prayers I was a different person. I could talk about the illness and I can talk any time to anyone about it now.

A quiet, reserved woman, Mrs Armstrong has gained tremendous inner strength in recent years. She now gets up in front of large crowds of people to tell her story:

> I can confidently tell them what positive thinking and prayers have done for me. I don't think I ever had any bitterness. On Ted's headstone it just says he died 'tragically on Remembrance Sunday'. It is only now I can say 'murdered'. But that is what they were.

Kathleen Armstrong believes that God brought her to work for the Barnabas Trust, a voluntary organisation in Enniskillen:

> In 1988 God planned a job for me in Barnabas. I was a community visitor for one year and I am still there as a voluntary craft supervisor. I love my job and it was meant for me. I feel very lonely at times, but helping the club members helps me, and they are all so good to me.

Spiritual Strength

There seems to be a definite thread running through the lives of many of those directly affected, and it has manifested itself as a spiritual strengthening.

David Bolton has seen many psychological responses, including periods of sadness and being withdrawn, forgetfulness, preoccupation, daydreaming, disturbed sleep and not eating properly. One woman, on holiday in Edinburgh when a ceremonial gun was fired from the walls of the Castle, dived to the ground in what psychiatrists call an 'as if' experience. However, David Bolton points out:

> In many ways it has been quite remarkable that so many people adjusted so much following the experience. I know that even now, ten years on, people still feel the hurt, the sadness and the outrage of it. But if you look at how many people have got back involved with their lives and got on with their lives, it really is quite remarkable.
>
> I don't believe I ever came across anybody whose faith was lost over Enniskillen. I have come across people whose faith was changed and in some way enriched in the long term.

While it would be wrong to generalise, and not all the
people who were injured or who lost relatives have found
this spiritual enrichment, it is evident that faith has
enabled many to come through some terrifyingly traumatic times.

10: Republican Own Goal?

With eleven members of Enniskillen's Protestant community dead, the sense of anger, hurt and vulnerability was felt by the wider Unionist community throughout Northern Ireland. As has been outlined in earlier chapters, the massacre also touched Nationalists on both sides of the Border. But what impact did it have on support for the IRA from within the Republican community?

Revulsion and condemnation were universal, with even Libya criticising the IRA through its news agency. But in common with the disgust felt by Fermanagh Catholics, many of whom had supported Sinn Féin in Council elections just two years earlier, the horror felt by huge numbers in the Republic devastated whatever support or even tolerance there had been towards the IRA there. In an interview with journalist David McKittrick in the London *Independent* newspaper a few days after the bombing, a senior member of the IRA's military command was quoted as saying:

> It will hurt us really badly there, more than anywhere else. We were trying to convince people there that what's happening in the North is a legitimate armed struggle.

The bombing also had a major impact on the IRA's support internationally, particularly in the United States where the Irish-American community had given vital moral support over the years. Irish-Americans had also, crucially, supported the IRA financially. Following the bombing, Dublin rock group U2 were in the US on their *Joshua Tree* tour. In one performance, lead singer Bono said these words over the backing music to 'Sunday, Bloody Sunday':

> I've had enough of Irish-Americans, who haven't been back to their country in twenty or thirty years, come up to me and talk about the resistance, the revolution back home and the *glory* of the revolution, and the *glory* of dying for the revolution. Fuck the revolution! They don't talk about the glory of *killing* for the revolution. . . . Where's the glory in bombing a Remembrance Day parade of old-age pensioners, the medals taken out and polished up for the day? Where's the glory in that? that leave them dying or crippled for life or dead under the rubble of the revolution, that the majority of the people in my country don't want. *No more!*

In *A History of Ulster* Jonathan Bardon points out that Bono's words were subsequently included in the film of the *Rattle and Hum* tour and says:

> These words were heard by millions and may have done more to discourage Irish-American financial support for the Provisional IRA than all the politicians' appeals put together.[1]

What appears to have hurt the Republican movement particularly was that the nature of the attack at Enniskillen allowed the British to portray the IRA as 'criminals'. The IRA's insistence that its struggle was a political one had been central in developing its strategy throughout the 1980s in particular. By 1987, Sinn Féin had developed into a political party with increasing electoral support. Despite its links with the IRA, its members were attracting more of the Nationalist vote in Northern Ireland than they had done for at least forty years, and were eating into the support normally enjoyed by the John-Hume-led Social Democratic and Labour Party (SDLP), which is committed to achieving a united Ireland by peaceful means and by agreement.

Sinn Féin members also worked hard at spreading their message abroad, so that they gained some measure of international acceptance.

1950s to 1970s War

The reaction to Enniskillen threatened to undermine Sinn Féin's work throughout the 1980s, which saw the party emerge as a co-ordinated political force, with a wide support base. By 1987, it was more successful than at any time since the 1950s, possibly even since Sinn Féin had split in the 1920s after partition.

A strong strain of Republicanism has always existed in this corner of Northern Ireland. Fermanagh came under attack in the 1950s IRA Border campaign. In 1955, a Sinn Féin prisoner, Philip Clarke, won the election in Fermanagh–South Tyrone, which was Enniskillen's constituency. He was later disqualified from holding the seat. Another prisoner, Thomas Mitchell, won the mid-Ulster seat in that year.

In an incident in 1957, two young IRA men were shot dead by the security forces in a botched raid on Brookeborough RUC barracks. The men, Feargal O'Hanlon from Monaghan, and Seán South from Garryowen, Co. Limerick, passed into Republican folklore and on the fortieth anniversary of their deaths in 1997 a stone memorial was unveiled by a group of Republicans at the site where they died. There were angry protests from local Unionists, some of whom had served in the B Specials, the part-time element in the RUC which was mainly Protestant. The 'B' men, as they were known, had repelled the raid.

The 1950s Border campaign fizzled out, but events in Northern Ireland at the end of the 1960s provided an opportunity to revitalise the IRA. The Northern Ireland Civil Rights Association (NICRA) had been set up to protest about discrimination against Catholics especially in the allocation of jobs and houses. NICRA's public protests resulted in community strife and unrest, with the two communities at each other's throats. When certain Nationalist areas in Belfast in particular came under physical attack from Loyalists, the IRA stepped in and played the role of defenders.

Having taken advantage of the situation to gain support, the IRA soon moved into offensive mode, and its energies during the 1970s were channelled mainly into an intense and sustained campaign of shootings and bombings of commercial and military targets. This campaign, aimed at physically forcing the British out of Ireland, continued relentlessly throughout the decade, with the military wing undoubtedly calling the shots. However, efforts were still going on to organise politically. Gerry Adams, now Sinn Féin president, points out the difficulty of organising politically with most of the members 'underground':

> You are always on the defensive. You need to have people who are out there within the community openly available and to be accountable to people. You cannot organise as effectively underground, and being underground uses up an awful lot of energy. If you don't want to go to Long Kesh [the Maze prison] or if you don't want to be killed, you are using a lot of energy in terms of just staying alive and staying safe.

Long-serving Fermanagh Sinn Féin member Paul Corrigan recalls the practical difficulties. Often he would be stopped in his car, or his house would be raided and he would be taken in for questioning:

> It was difficult even to hold meetings because we would be raided and held. I don't think there was an RUC barracks in Fermanagh I didn't see the inside of.

In the 1970s, while the IRA continued its war, the political arena was left to the new SDLP and old-style Nationalists. The Fermanagh–South Tyrone constituency had a Nationalist majority, but unless there was an agreed Nationalist candidate, the seat was often won by a Unionist. Local Nationalist solicitor Frank McManus held it in the early 1970s, but Unionists regained it in 1974 through Ulster Unionist leader Harry West. West had been Minister for Agriculture in the Northern Ireland parliament at Stormont. The Unionist-dominated parliament had been suspended by the British in 1972 when its members refused to accept the loss of powers over security.

Later in 1974, Harry West lost the seat to Frank Maguire, a publican from Lisnaskea in the staunchly Republican South Fermanagh. Maguire held the seat for much of the decade, while consistently refusing to attend the Westminster parliament. His stance was in keeping with the Republican tradition of abstentionism although he was not a member of Sinn Féin. Throughout the century Sinn Féin had refused to attend the British parliament, which its members did not recognise as having jurisdiction over any part of Ireland. Neither did they recognise Dáil Éireann, the Irish parliament, set up following the agreement with Britain which had allowed for partition.

Prison Protest

Sinn Féin did not contest elections in the 1970s, but it was then that the seeds for later success were sown. As the IRA's campaign continued, more and more volunteers were imprisoned. Republican inmates in the Maze prison had been on a collision course with the British Government since 1976 when Labour Secretary of State Roy Mason had refused to grant prisoner Kieran Nugent 'special category status'. He was the first Provisional IRA man convicted of terrorism to be denied the status, which would have acknowledged him as a political prisoner. In response, he refused to wear a prison uniform — which would have labelled him as an ordinary criminal — wrapping himself in a blanket instead. Inside the prison's cell blocks — known as the H-blocks because of their shape — the protests continued. More men went 'on the blanket' and engaged in the 'dirty protest', which involved rubbing human excrement on the walls. Having been interned without trial in the early 1970s, Gerry Adams was back behind bars in the latter part of the decade. He recalls:

> We were going through a fairly major review of where Sinn Féin was going to build a party. When I was re-arrested I ended up for a short period in the H-block of Long Kesh and I came very much face to face with the reality of the blanket protest which had gone on for some time now, and in Armagh women's prison.

Adams had been charged with IRA membership, a charge which he says 'was thrown out of court', and at the next Sinn Féin ard-fheis (party conference) he was elected vice-president of the party:

> We continued our work to rebuild the party, or as I would describe it, bring the party back to its roots and develop it as a campaigning party. I myself was very influenced by what I had seen in the blocks, so I was able to bring some of that experience to bear.

Part of that reorganisation was the formation of a 'Prisoner of War' department, which formulated five demands based around prison conditions and political status.

Hunger Strike

In October 1980, as the campaign continued to face an inflexible response to its demands, seven prisoners embarked on a hunger strike which did not last. In 1981 another hunger strike began. By this time Britain had a new Conservative Prime Minister, Margaret Thatcher, who quickly made it clear that there would be no concession on political status.

Around the same time, Frank Maguire, the Fermanagh–South Tyrone MP and a staunch supporter of the prisoners' campaign, died, and the notion arose of nominating a prisoner for election. The subject of whether to fight elections or not was always a potentially divisive matter in Republican ranks. But the 1981 Westminster by-election was too good an opportunity to overlook. An agreed Nationalist candidate would be sure to win in Fermanagh–South Tyrone, and the election would be contested not by Sinn Féin as such, but by hunger-striker Bobby Sands who had agreed to fight on an 'anti-H-block' ticket.

In the end it came down to a straight fight between Bobby Sands and Harry West who came out of political retirement. The Sands campaign was brilliantly run, focusing on the humanitarian issue, while Protestants could see Sands only as an IRA gunman. The turnout at the poll was a massive 86 per cent, with the hunger striker getting 30,492 votes to West's 29,046. Unionists were shaken, and West declared, 'Now we know the type of people we are living amongst.'

After sixty-six days on hunger strike, Bobby Sands was the first of the prisoners to starve to death. His election agent at the April contest, Owen Carron, fought the resulting by-election in August the same year on the same issue, this time against a new Unionist candidate, Ken Maginnis. The turnout went up to almost 89 per cent, and while Maginnis held up the Unionist vote, Carron actually polled over 700 more votes than Sands had.

Carron, a former teacher from Macken, Co. Fermanagh, remained as MP for the area for two years. At the British general election of June 1983, he fought the seat for Sinn Féin, who by now had embraced what Gerry Adams describes as 'electoralism'. This time there was no free run on the Nationalist side, however, with Carron opposed by the SDLP. Unionist Ken Maginnis took the seat, which he still holds.

Those within the Republican movement who had always propagated ideology were learning the value of electoral success. Following the Sands victory, prisoners decided to contest the general election held in the Republic. Paddy Agnew was elected in Louth, and Kieran Doherty won a seat in Cavan–Monaghan, just across the Border from Fermanagh.

Throughout the summer, a total of twenty-three prisoners went on hunger strike, some replacing others who
had fasted to death. They included not only IRA prisoners, but also men from the Irish National Liberation Army
(INLA) a lesser-known smaller Republican faction, also
carrying out a military campaign. With some having come
off the protest in need of medical treatment and other
families threatening to intervene, the hunger strike ended
in October 1981.

By then, ten prisoners had died and Northern Ireland
had faced a summer of street violence as emotions
reached boiling point on both sides. All shades of Nationalist opinion, as well as the Catholic Church, were crying
out for a humanitarian solution, but Margaret Thatcher
saw it purely in terms of a law and order issue and would
not be moved. In Enniskillen, protesters tried to break
down the door of the Townhall when a false rumour
spread that the British Prime Minister was inside.

It was the task of Margaret Thatcher's press secretary,
Sir Bernard Ingham, to get the message across that she
would not be moved:

> What she said in the hunger strike was that these people
> have a choice. But don't think that they are going to move
> me by starving themselves to death. If that is the turn in
> which terrorism takes them, they better get on with it.
> She expected it would be manipulated by them, but the
> message I was told to get over to the media was that it
> wouldn't work.

The intransigence of Mrs Thatcher was credited with
gaining a wave of new sympathy for the Republican
movement. Now an Independent Nationalist representative in Fermanagh, Councillor Tony McPhillips joined
Sinn Féin as a result of the hunger strike issue in 1981
when he was just 19 years old. He recalls his sense of
outrage:

> With the advent of the first hunger strike in 1980, my be-
> liefs began to undergo rapid change. The following hunger

strike in 1981 had a profound effect on me and convinced me that a more radical and involved approach was required from young people like myself.

The selfless sacrifices of those ten young men, I believe, inspired a generation of young Nationalists to accept that the only solution to this conflict lay in a total British disengagement from the North, and so was born my involvement in the rise in public support for the Republican movement. The election of Bobby Sands and subsequently that of Owen Carron gave a great feeling of Nationalist unity, all of us with the one aim in mind. Throughout the early to mid-1980s that support was strongly reflected at election after election, particularly here in Fermanagh. Fermanagh had once again played its part in a political watershed.

However, in the Protestant community, the reaction to the hunger strikes was entirely different: the general view was that the Government could not give in to the blackmail of the IRA and that, however regrettable the deaths were, these men were responsible for taking their own lives. The Protestant community in Fermanagh–South Tyrone received a jolt at the massive support for Bobby Sands. Ulster Unionist Councillor in Enniskillen, Raymond Ferguson, says that a minority of Unionists may have expected the result:

> But the rest of them were astounded that the Catholic community could come in and support Bobby Sands. But they did. The Sands election was a huge shock to the Unionist community.

Protestants' traditional old fears of deep-rooted Catholic tolerance for the IRA's method of getting a united Ireland resurfaced. It even appears to have produced more of a hurt than the bombing in 1987, when the anger was focused directly at those responsible — the IRA. Presbyterian minister the Rev. David Cupples explains that when Catholics sympathised with their Protestant neighbours after the bomb, that was taken at face value and accepted as sincere. However,

What people say to me is that when Bobby Sands was elected every single last person got out and voted that day. When hardy came to hardy, almost every single Catholic and Nationalist in this county went out and voted for Sinn Féin, for an IRA man, and they said that shows where their ultimate sympathy really lies. The number of times that was mentioned to me in the first few years that I was here really surprised me and seemed to have a much more damaging effect and to have much more power to make Protestants mistrust the Catholic community than the Enniskillen bomb.

The spectacular successes at various polls removed any doubt that many Sinn Féiners had about electoralism. Gerry Adams preached for an 'electoral strategy', rather than 'electoral intervention' with the vote subsiding after a particular crisis subsided. He says:

What we needed was a strategy which is about popularising the struggle, radicalising the struggle and building a political party which is relevant to people in their daily lives, which makes Irish Republicanism relevant to people in their daily lives.

Ballot Box and Armalite

Buoyed by the Sands success, Sinn Féin quickly embraced electoralism. At the party's ard-fheis, leading member Danny Morrison stated:

Who here really believes we can win the war through the ballot box? But will anyone here object if, with a ballot paper in one hand and the Armalite in the other, we take power in Ireland?

It is a remark that has come back to haunt Sinn Féin many times. Adams says:

I winced when I heard it. I knew it was going to come back to revisit us. I think in fairness to Danny Morrison his remark has been taken out of context because he was not seeking to make it a declaration of Republican policy or strategy, he was seeking instead to convince Republican delegates to the ard-fheis to take up a new position, to move forward. But he did so in a way that he left himself open to misrepresentation.

The 'new position' is what others describe as the development of the political wing. Sinn Féin calls it 'electoralism', claiming that the military part of the Republican struggle is also political, but that the two are separate. However, the validity of this argument is not accepted in many quarters, where it is believed that Sinn Féin is not a separate party but part and parcel of the IRA. Unionists continue to refer to them as 'Sinn Féin-IRA'.

In the British general election of 1983, Sinn Féin gained widespread support at the polls for the first time, with Gerry Adams defeating long-standing SDLP MP Gerry Fitt in West Belfast. By the time of the local elections of 1985, Sinn Féin's percentage vote had slipped, although the party still managed to gain fifty-nine seats in councils across Northern Ireland. It was particularly successful in Fermanagh, winning eight of the twenty-three seats in Enniskillen on its first attempt.

This left Sinn Féin level with the Ulster Unionists as the largest party, but the make-up of the rest of the Council saw Nationalists in a majority of 13–10. At the first meeting of the newly elected Council, the SDLP voted with Sinn Féin to elect Paul Corrigan the first Sinn Féin chairman of any of Northern Ireland's twenty-six district councils.

The party had arrived as a political force, but there was still some unease within the ranks. There was a split, and dissidents opposed to ending abstentionism went on to form Republican Sinn Féin under Ruairí Ó Brádaigh.

Fermanagh District Council

The involvement of Sinn Féin in Fermanagh District Council was especially controversial in the early days. In the election campaign Sinn Féin had stated that it 'unambiguously supported the armed struggle'. British

Government Ministers, who had governed Northern Ireland directly since the suspension of Stormont, refused to meet Council delegations which had Sinn Féin members.

In the summer of 1985, RUC Constable Robert Gilliland was killed in a bombing at Kinawley on the Fermanagh border. Paul Corrigan reiterated his position as one of 'unequivocal support of the IRA and its armed struggle'.

In November, Prime Minister Margaret Thatcher and Taoiseach Garret FitzGerald signed the Anglo–Irish Agreement, which established an inter-governmental conference. For the first time, the Government of the Republic of Ireland would have a say on the internal affairs of Northern Ireland. Unionists withdrew from the Council in protest.

In 1986 when Monaghan IRA man Seamus McElwaine was shot dead by the SAS, Paul Corrigan travelled to Monaghan to join thousands of mourners at his funeral. He publicly lauded McElwaine, describing him as a great friend of Fermanagh.

Nevertheless, Gerry Adams insists that in the mid-1980s Sinn Féin and the IRA were developing separately:

> For its part the IRA was doing what the IRA was doing, so you had a separate development. Then there were those of us who were increasingly taken by electoralism, which is only one aspect of what Sinn Féin was doing. There is the need for international outreach, the need to build up your publicity outlets. We were obviously attracting more people to the party, building the party.

Since the 1920s, there had been sporadic expression of Republicanism through military methods. Adams explains:

> Republican activism has mainly manifested itself in militarism or in armed actions. While they are clearly political, and while those involved are both political and in some cases very politically conscious, it was generally the militaristic tendency who was in the ascendancy.

Now, in the mid-1980s, there was an organised expression of Republicanism in an unarmed way.

Setback for the Republican Movement

In this context, the nature of the Enniskillen bombing must surely have been a major setback for the movement. Gerry Adams answers the question frankly:

> I have to deal with Enniskillen in the first instance in what it meant to the people who were killed. All the other elements of it have to be secondary. I think the operation was wrong in its conception as well as in its execution. Fair enough, the IRA have explained that their target was the guard of honour, the UDR. I accept that the intentions of the IRA were not to kill civilians; I accept that their intentions were not to attack a group of people attending a commemoration, but that is the reality of what it turned out to be. So I think both in its conception and in its execution it was a disaster.
>
> I make the point very consciously that what the IRA did was wrong.
>
> My human response to what happened was not affected by whether it was good or bad for Sinn Féin. The first thing is that people who had gathered to pay homage were victims of a Republican action which should not have occurred.
>
> I certainly regretted very much the hurt that was caused and I have expressed on a number of occasions my sense of regret for the hurt which Republicans have inflicted.

He points out that the effect of Enniskillen was 'to depress and upset many Republican activists':

> I have long-standing friends who have suffered grievously in the struggle, people living in Sligo, people living in Leitrim, people living in Dublin, people living in Meath who I know as long-standing comrades. These people worked very, very hard and I remember they were just very upset by what occurred.

Chairman of the Council

While many Republicans reflected in private on the aftermath of Enniskillen, there was no such luxury for the high-profile chairman of Fermanagh District Council, who had to deal with public perceptions. In a statement issued on the evening of the bombing, Paul Corrigan said that he and other Sinn Féin councillors were shocked by the deaths and horrific injuries:

> Sinn Féin is in a vulnerable position because of its opposition to British rule and does not expect to escape the consequences.

A Council committee meeting due to be held the following afternoon was adjourned, and a battery of television cameras and journalists waited outside as councillors emerged from Enniskillen Townhall. Initially, journalists directed their questions at Unionist Councillor Raymond Ferguson who snapped, 'You know what Unionists think. You should be talking to Sinn Féin; they're the guilty men.'

Ferguson remembers the mood following the meeting:

> By the Monday, anger had built up as the enormity of the event came through. People had time to take account of what exactly had happened, what they had done and who they had done it to. There was nothing to redeem it in any way. It was the most atrocious event to date that happened in the IRA campaign. Everybody was exceptionally annoyed and when Sinn Féin came into the Council chamber they were clearly uneasy. When we came out of the chamber the press were all around and they started asking what we thought of it. Well, we were the people who were the victims, we were the innocent parties, so it did annoy me that they were coming to us when they had the people who were justifying it about to come down the Townhall steps.

It was an impossible situation for Paul Corrigan, who was pursued by reporters as he walked the one hundred yards to his car. He remembers remaining silent and refusing to answer a barrage of questions:

> I thought in the circumstances there was no point. I hadn't run away from the Council meeting. The bombing was as much a shock to me and it shouldn't have happened; but

I had already given a statement expressing my regret and sympathy for those killed and injured.

I felt I was hounded by other councillors and hounded by the press. I was as surprised and shocked as anyone else by what had happened, but I didn't do it. Any thinking person knew I had nothing to do with it, yet they vented their anger on me.

He received numerous abusive phone calls and letters, including some death threats. Some came from England and the US. His critics also made much of the fact that his wife, Patricia, who was a nurse at the Erne hospital, did not report in on the day of the bomb. In fact, she was away in Sligo on a day off, and Protestant nurses who were not in the area were not there either. Mrs Corrigan also received hate mail. Her husband recalls:

It all added to the trauma and difficulty for my family. It was a very trying period. I was being personally attacked for something I did not do.

While accepting that because he had supported the IRA's right to conduct its campaign, people would blame him for what happened, Mr Corrigan points out:

Just because I supported the IRA's right, that doesn't mean I approved of every action they took. I said at the time it shouldn't have happened. It couldn't be condoned.

He recalls other atrocities in Fermanagh, and asks:

Where Nationalists were murdered, some by members of the security forces, should Unionists stand equally condemned?

At the December 1987 meeting of Fermanagh District Council, the SDLP proposed a motion of no confidence in Paul Corrigan. It was passed with Unionist backing, but he refused to resign. He explains:

I felt it was political expediency. I personally hadn't done anything wrong in the role of chairman.

He was supported by his party whose national chairperson, Mitchel McLaughlin, travelled from Derry to

Enniskillen, and sat in on the difficult Council meeting.

Paul Corrigan subsequently had a heart by-pass operation and his sons now run the family farm.

Sinn Féin's representation on Fermanagh Council dropped significantly, and in the 1989 elections representation was halved to four seats. While this drop can be partly explained by the breakaway of the Ó Brádaigh faction, the Enniskillen bomb clearly put both the IRA and Sinn Féin under serious pressure.

The Investigation

Not one person has ever been charged with any offence in connection with the bombing, in spite of one of the most intensive and lengthy investigations ever carried out by the RUC.

Enniskillen sits in 'L' division in the RUC's administrative structure, and the Criminal Investigation Department in the entire division was staffed by nine detectives, including a chief inspector, an inspector, a sergeant and six constables. Another twenty-four, including four senior officers, were brought in, with a detective superintendent heading the investigation.

In the hours after the bombing, while RUC and British Army personnel were sealing off the area to check for further bombs, a briefing was already being held in police headquarters in Enniskillen, the heavily fortified old barracks, which itself had been attacked by the IRA in 1985.

At the bomb site, a meticulous search was held. Thirty uniformed men in boiler suits sifted through the rubble looking for clues. After three days they had filled twenty skips with several tonnes of material, which was sent off for detailed examination at the Northern Ireland Forensic Science Laboratory in Belfast. Scientists discovered that the bomb had been detonated by a pre-set timer, and not by an electronic signal. This allowed the British Army to dismiss IRA claims that Army electronic surveillance equipment had accidentally set the bomb off. However, it was of limited practical use in the bid to learn the identity of the bombers.

Back in the major incident room at Enniskillen, a total of 269 statements were recorded and 275 enquiries were followed up. Many witnesses came forward with information, and ten well-known Republicans from the area were arrested and brought to Gough Barracks in Armagh for questioning. But those detained were released after several days.

Further information came from the Garda Síochána, both formally and informally, as the RUC had built up a working relationship with Irish police officers in Donegal, Cavan and Monaghan, where it was suspected the IRA operation had been planned and carried out from.

Nevertheless, the security forces came no nearer to catching the bomber. This failure is consistent with the difficulty the security forces have in Fermanagh. Firstly, the IRA is a sophisticated and modern guerrilla organisation, whose operations are usually well planned. A team carrying out an operation, known as an 'Active Service Unit', covers its tracks well and it is rare for any evidence to be uncovered. Secondly, any information that is forthcoming from people in the area has to be confidential because of fear of reprisals. It is unlikely that people would give evidence in court.

Ulster Unionist MP Ken Maginnis says that in areas such as South Fermanagh and South Armagh, the terrorist movement has better 'internal security':

> It has more to do with family connections and a stable population, unlike Belfast which has a transient population. Family connections bind a community together in Fermanagh. It is very hard to give up somebody who is married to your favourite cousin or whose father and mother were best friends with your father and mother. It is more of a mafia in Fermanagh.

In spite of the genuine revulsion of the Catholic community in general, it was highly unlikely that the appeals from the Catholic Church would touch the few who might know something about the Enniskillen operation.

The geography of the area was also in the bombers' favour. Fermanagh has seventy-five miles of land border with the Republic, most of it in isolated and bleak countryside. Access to the farmhouses dotted around the land is often from long concrete lanes, which at times run into other farms. The notion that such a border could be sealed, as some Unionist politicians have suggested, is nonsense. However, its existence provides a tangled web of roads perfect for terrorists to slip into.

In addition to army undercover patrols, the main method of restricting the IRA's movement in pre-ceasefire days was permanent vehicle checkpoints on strategic routes. British soldiers, based in reinforced shelters, would check cars passing. Computers inside could give information on specific registrations, and vehicles would often be stopped and searched. However, the checkpoints themselves become a target for bombing or shooting missions.

Border Haven

Many Unionists view the Republic's Border counties as a 'haven for terrorists'. Unionist MP Ken Maginnis says that Fermanagh's proximity to the Border means that much of the IRA's planning can take place in the Republic, undetected by the northern security forces. This view was shared by Margaret Thatcher. According to her press secretary, Sir Bernard Ingham, Mrs Thatcher regarded the Republic as a 'bolt hole' for the IRA and this led to a difficult relationship with the Irish Taoiseach in 1987, Charles Haughey. Ingham says:

> Her relationship with him was difficult. She didn't believe that they took terrorism as seriously as they ought to have.

This was particularly evident at the time of Enniskillen, says Sir Bernard:

> Well it was close to the Border, wasn't it? I think she had two points: that you can't easily defeat terrorism when it

has support within the community and, indeed, when they have a bolt-hole south of the border.

The Thatcher administration's perception of the Border as a bolt-hole for terrorists escaping from Northern Ireland is shared by many Unionists. It is, however, hotly denied by most people in the Republic, who often point out that their police resources are stretched in other parts of the country because of the number of gardaí deployed along the Border. Indeed, people in the Republic are often offended by the notion that there is general support for the IRA in their country. As rock singer Bono pointed out in his impassioned statement in the US following the Enniskillen bomb, the IRA's campaign is something 'the majority of the people in my country don't want'.

Despite the awfulness of Enniskillen, it is clear that Mrs Thatcher did not regard it as a 'turning point'. Ingham says:

> Events like Enniskillen will contribute to the ultimate defeat of the IRA, but I don't think in 1987 anybody deluded themselves that it was going to happen then. She knew we had been through so many turning points in Northern Ireland.

Nevertheless, at the end of November 1987, forty people were arrested after a series of arms finds on both sides of the Border.

The Republican Mood

While Mrs Thatcher's condemnation will hardly have annoyed Republicans greatly, the depth of disapproval from so many other quarters clearly hurt. However, as time went on, many rank-and-file Republicans began to think of all the atrocities carried out against Nationalists: such as the Loyalist bombing of McGurk's Bar in 1972, when sixteen people had been killed; or Bloody Sunday 1972, when the British Army opened fire on an anti-internment march, killing thirteen unarmed men. Many felt that there had not been such intense condemnation of atrocities committed against their community.

Moreover, hard-line Republicans would be inclined to transfer the blame to what they saw as the core cause of all conflict — the simple presence of the British in Ireland. Gerry Adams says:

> People like me cannot be expected to take on the guilt. As we have seen even this summer, there is an attempt to do that in the politics of the last atrocity, by conscious attempt to guilt trip those who vote for our party. And that is despite the fact that we made it very clear that our party is not the IRA, and people voting for us are not voting for the IRA.
>
> I think grief, trauma, death, destruction, conflict — how do you end it? You end it by getting to the core of it.

He feels that events in 1987 'strengthened the attempts to isolate Sinn Féin'. In 1988, the British Government introduced a broadcasting ban, which effectively banned television and radio stations from using the voices of Sinn Féin representatives in interviews. A total ban on interviewing Sinn Féin members and members of similar organisations was already in existence in the Republic of Ireland.

However, according to Gerry Adams, even as these events were happening, influential leaders in Sinn Féin were beginning what he calls 'building a peace strategy':

> There was some outreach work with the SDLP and with John Hume; but some of us had come to the decision that Sinn Féin needed to be part of building a peace settlement on clearly stated principles which are now in everyday language.

Adams' own cousin, Kieran Murphy, was mutilated by the infamous Loyalist killer gang, the Shankill Butchers; his sister was six months pregnant when her husband was shot dead by the British Army; and Adams himself was shot and wounded by Loyalists in one of several attacks:

> People may say, 'What do you expect?' But I am prepared to forgive the people who did this. Even if they show no

remorse. I don't have the emotion to waste, hatred is a wasted emotion. So what I am saying is, let's move on, we need to be reconciled.

The way to prevent events like Enniskillen is to get inclusive settlement. I think my great challenge in life is to try and create the conditions in which these tragedies will never happen again, because there have been numerous since Enniskillen and numerous before Enniskillen.

No Turning Point

The year of 1987 had been a bad one for the IRA: exactly six months before Enniskillen, it had lost eight of its best men, shot dead at Loughgall, Co. Armagh, in an SAS ambush. They had been on their way to bomb the village's RUC station, but forty SAS men were waiting, some of them inside the station. Among those killed was Jim Lynagh, one of the IRA's élite who was also known to the security forces along the Fermanagh–Monaghan Border.

Whether the Enniskillen bombing was in some part a retaliation is a matter of conjecture. In any case, the Republican war machine showed no immediate sign of letting up. With arms being supplied by Libya, the IRA was now more heavily armed than ever, and in 1988 IRA atrocities continued to cause death, suffering and horror in south-west Ulster and throughout Northern Ireland. Hopes were soon dashed that somehow the IRA had stooped so low at Enniskillen that its members would show remorse.

Ten years after Enniskillen, Sinn Féin is at one of its highest points ever. The party has recaptured the broad Republican vote — in the mid-Ulster constituency at the 1997 British general election Martin McGuinness won the seat with 20,000 votes. Sinn Féin as a political party is as strong now as it has been since the 1920s.

One Republican I spoke to said that to understand why the Enniskillen tragedy was not a turning point, it was necessary to understand the nature of the Republican movement. While there is tremendous discipline within the ranks, it is not some monolith, moving solidly in unison:

> It doesn't work like that. It can be a conspiratorial hotch-potch which moves slowly with agreement. Republican leaders are very calculating in their way.

It must also be said that there is a strand within Republicanism that will never be persuaded to forsake military means and move towards the political path.

What becomes clear from an analysis of the bombing of Enniskillen and its aftermath in the context of Northern Ireland's turbulent history, is that no one single event, even one as agonising as Enniskillen, can be a 'turning point' in itself. However, in the late 1980s, it was one of a number of events which forced many people to do some soul-searching.

---

1 Bardon, J. (1992): *A History of Ulster*, Belfast: Blackstaff Press.

11: Remember and Change

After the Enniskillen bomb, the Church of Ireland Bishop of Clogher, the Right Rev. Brian Hannon, said that the tragedy had strengthened the hand of moderates because it showed where extremism could lead. Two weeks later, at the rearranged Remembrance Sunday service, Archbishop Robin Eames preached a sermon on the theme 'Blessed are the peacemakers'. At a time when there might have been bitter recrimination, people were looking for signs of hope.

Fermanagh

Fermanagh is a county with a rich mixture of cultures and divisions, old and modern ways, and warm people. The stunning lakeland, a mecca for fishermen, also has its social problems though, such as high unemployment and poor housing. However, there has never been any strong socialist or labour movement in Northern Ireland, with politics dominated by the wider Constitutional issue.

To the east of Fermanagh are the more densely populated counties and industrial Belfast, whose people often seem harsh and arrogant to the easygoing Fermanagh person. North-west lie rival Tyrone and Derry (as a northern Protestant born in the 1950s, I have always called it Derry, as opposed to Londonderry, which many insist on). Fermanagh folk have never had any great affinity with Derry, seeing its people as distant and complaining.

To the south and west of Fermanagh are the counties

of the Republic of Ireland. Neither side has fully come to terms with the arbitrary cut of partition. These are counties which Protestants regard with a mixture of suspicion and fondness, while Catholics view them as neighbours.

There is a certain laid-back feeling about Fermanagh, which sometimes translates into an attitude of 'all the world's odd but us.' However, the two tribes, fairly evenly split numerically, cling to their beliefs privately but tenaciously. On the Protestant side, the Church of Ireland is predominant, with staunch traditional family support for the Orange and Black institutions. There are also numerous evangelical and fundamentalist congregations with a strong passion for their Christianity. However easygoing many of the Protestant farming folk appear, they will always dig their heels in on a point of principle. The siege mentality is never more apparent than in the Protestant community living on the Border.

The equally devout Roman Catholic community holds fast to its Nationalist aspirations, particularly in the south of the county, which is mainly Republican at heart. Large areas have never come to terms with being sliced off from what they regard as their natural hinterland in counties such as Monaghan.

The deep-rooted rivalry manifests itself in turnouts at elections of anything up to 90 per cent, with the electorate voting along sectarian lines. However, community relations are good and two neighbouring farmers who, by night, have no difficulty in justifying taking the other's life, will show unbelievable generosity of spirit in helping each other out by day. Privately, both sides admit that what they have in common is greater than what divides them — the outsider who slanders one Fermanagh man insults them all.

The Divisions

It is a sad paradox: a people who feel so much in common, yet are so divided. Hope is there, but in working for peace and reconciliation the differences cannot be ignored. These divisions have resulted in the area being a battleground for the past twenty-seven years and longer. The IRA campaign has been largely directed against the security forces. Almost all part-time members of the RUC and UDR murdered have been Protestants, many of them farmers with no family old enough to take over the farm. This has led to suggestions of Protestant genocide and ethnic cleansing. A number of Protestant families have either sold their property and moved to Scotland, or left their farms dormant and moved closer 'inland', further away from the Fermanagh Border.

Claims of ethnic cleansing are strenuously denied by local Nationalists, who in turn feel hard done by. They claim that their culture has never been recognised and that they have been systematically discriminated against throughout the history of the state.

Perceptions heighten the divisions, and there is clearly a lack of trust. Those working for reconciliation recognise that the best way to break down distrust is to bring people together, and allow them to learn about each other's way of life.

Community Together

While the strife continued after the Enniskillen bomb, many good things also came about in its aftermath. According to Unionist Councillor Raymond Ferguson, 'The community has held together and shown its determination to get on together.'

Indeed, the bonds forged between ordinary Catholics and Protestants in Enniskillen in 1987 remain intact. Following the tragedy, expression from both sides was often united through an organisation called Enniskillen Together, formed after two young men, Edwin Graham and Pauric Dolan, arranged vigils and meetings in the town library. Having provided an initial channel for expressing their revulsion, the movement went on to bring townspeople together in practical ways. In its early years, efforts were concentrated on three fronts: arts and culture, education and churches. Later, such events as community festivals were organised.

A churches group was formed, where lay people could get together and talk about each other's tradition and learn from their differences. The Enniskillen Together Churches Group organises a service each year during the week of prayer for Christian unity.

Another section of Enniskillen Together hived off and considered education. This group eventually led to the formation of an integrated school in the town. Education in Northern Ireland is still segregated to a large extent, but Protestant and Catholic parents in Enniskillen now have the choice of having their children educated with children from the other tradition. Enniskillen Together still exists in a low-key way, and makes a valuable contribution behind the scenes — in conciliation over contentious parades, for example.

The integrated primary school has been successful, and in recent years a new integrated college opened as the logical next step to take pupils on to secondary education. There are also very good relationships among all the other schools in Enniskillen, across the community divide. Even before the Enniskillen bomb, the Western Education and Library Board had implemented a programme called 'Education in Mutual Understanding'. This saw Protestant and Catholic schools co-operating on a range of projects, including visits to schools in England, in the Republic of Ireland and in Continental Europe. In the aftermath of the bombing, these ties proved extremely important and were strengthened as time went on.

Other formal efforts also continue to bring people together. The Canadian government set up the 'Marie Wilson Voyage of Hope' scheme, which provides funds for young people from schools in Fermanagh to travel to Canada to live with families and learn about Canadian culture. The scheme, named in honour of the youngest of the Enniskillen victims, sends different Fermanagh teenagers on the 'voyage' each summer. As mentioned in

Chapter 7, a British Government scheme, the Spirit of Enniskillen Trust, sends young people from Northern Ireland abroad to study conflict situations and see how different traditions have learned to live together.

There is, of course, some opposition to this, some of it based on ideological objections to bringing Protestants and Catholics together. Others feel that it is artificial to force people together like this; and some say that these measures are not needed as the people of Enniskillen have always got on well together anyway.

As someone who was born and brought up in Enniskillen, I can recall many cases of informal cross-community links which do not happen in other areas. Even boys who play football in mixed teams come into contact with people of a different religion, and those contacts prove invaluable in many cases in later life.

The polarisation may not be as great in Enniskillen as in other areas of Northern Ireland, but the circumstances of the past twenty-seven years have forced people in all towns into ghettos. Those involved in the work of getting people of all ages together across the divide are doing valuable work.

Ceasefire Brings Funding

The work of reconciliation was given a boost in 1994, following the announcement of the first IRA ceasefire. The then European Commission President, Jacques Delors, announced a special package of funding for Northern Ireland to be spent specifically on peace and reconciliation work. Partnerships involving public and community representatives across the spectrum were set up in each of the twenty-six district council areas in Northern Ireland to administer the funding. In October 1996, the Fermanagh District Partnership held a conference in Enniskillen called 'Remember and Change'.

The conference concluded that we should try to reach a point where we remember the past, out of respect and acknowledgement, while simultaneously reaching a determination to change. The chairman of the Partnership is David Bolton, the social worker who has been so close to the situation in Enniskillen (although this role is technically unconnected with that work). He explains:

> The tension between the need for justice and the need for mercy could be accommodated by accepting that we need both.

In his article in *When a Community Weeps*, David Bolton writes:

> On a wider front, the ability to adjust following a disaster is also about community self-confidence and its ability to transform what has been a tragedy into an opportunity for growth. Enniskillen has shown much evidence of this, with the town itself being the subject of many new commercial and architectural developments. Local people have a sense of self-confidence which was not there before. Having been in the eye of the media storm, it has become very used to visitors in the town, and many good things have been done among young people, enabling mutual understanding. Not everyone has been part of these developments, however, nor does everyone wish to be, and it is important to ensure that such improvements are at least open to everyone, even if not everyone wishes to be part of them. In the early days, the efforts were put into maintaining the community as it ran perilously close to disintegration. The efforts have now become focused on development.[1]

The Future

Enniskillen has come through its troubled day in 1987 extremely well. But in writing this book, the one thing that I found unnerving was the realisation that there is still the potential in Northern Ireland for more Enniskillens. It seems remarkable that in a society that has suffered so much, we have not quite reached a point where such an awful event can be ruled out. It may seem like a cliché, but the simple fact is that we must learn to live together. We must find agreement, including a political settlement, that allows this generation and future generations to share this land in a peaceful way, fully recognising the richness of both traditions.

---

1   Bolton, D. (1988): 'The Threat to Belonging in Enniskillen' in E.S. Zinner and M.B. Williams (Eds), *When a Community Weeps. Case Studies in Group Survivorship*, Washington DC: Taylor and Frances (forthcoming).